ar of

Edit

D0964135

Grammar of
the Edit

SECOND EDITION

Roy Thompson

Christopher J. Bowen

ELSEVIER

AMSTERDAM • BOSTON • HEIDELBERG • LONDON
NEW YORK • OXFORD • PARIS • SAN DIEGO
SAN FRANCISCO • SINGAPORE • SYDNEY • TOKYO
Focal Press is an imprint of Elsevier

Focal
Press

Focal Press is an imprint of Elsevier
30 Corporate Drive, Suite 400, Burlington, MA 01803, USA
Linacre House, Jordan Hill, Oxford OX2 8DP, UK

Library of Congress Cataloging-in-Publication Data
Application submitted

British Library Cataloguing-in-Publication Data
A catalogue record for this book is available from the British Library.

ISBN: 978-0-240-52120-6

For information on all Focal Press publications
visit our website at www.elsevierdirect.com

09 10 11 12   5 4 3 2 1

Printed in the United States of America

Contents

Acknowledgments

I wish to thank my editors at Focal Press, Elinor Actipis and Michele Cronin, for presenting me with the wonderful opportunity to write the second edition of this time honored text, *Grammar of the Edit*. Of course, this would not be possible without the ground work done by Mr. Roy Thompson on the first edition. I hope that this revised version continues to inform and inspire all those readers who are just beginning their creative journey into the world of editing motion pictures.

As an educator today, I wish to acknowledge the positive impact that my instructors at Brandeis University and Boston University had on me during my own higher education. The broad scope of the Liberal Arts was great preparation for the specific focus and technical craftsmanship that come with the field of film production. I present these same values to my own students and I thank them collectively for all they brought to me.

As a media professional today, I wish to thank my many colleagues and clients who have helped me to continue learning with each new project undertaken.

I am also grateful for the advice offered by several generous peers in the preparation of this second edition—Joey Goodsell, Norman Hollyn, Jane Jackson, and Catherine Sellars.

Additionally, I would like to thank my on-camera talent for their time on this project—Wendy Chao, Hannah Kurth, Alexander Scott, Stacy Shreffler, Eliza Smith, and Rachael Swain. All photographs are by the author, as are the line art diagrams and many of the illustrations. I must offer my thanks and appreciation to my co-illustrator, Jean Sharpe, whose distinct style and generous contributions make this text a better learning tool. Also, I offer a note of kind thanks to Mary James for her advice and assistance.

Lastly, I acknowledge my family for their support and offer extra special thanks to Rachael Swain who has been there through the thick and thin of it all and really helped pull all the pieces together.

This book is for all people who wish to learn the basics about editing film and video. I hope you have fun and enjoy the ride. If you would like to learn more about the topic, find additional resources, or learn more about the author, please visit the author's website www.fellswaycreatives.com.

For my mother

Introduction

Every motion picture you see and television drama you watch has been edited. Every commercial, news report, and talk show has been edited. Almost every presentation of motion imagery, whether it is fiction, non-fiction, or a melding of the two, has been edited — cut down, re-ordered, padded out, massaged, sweetened, and tweaked — to derive the final presentation version. That final version may be exactly what the creators set out to make or it may be entirely different in feel, tempo, information, and emotional impact, but no matter what, the editor helps make it so. It is, then, the job of the editor to take the materials created during production and manipulate them to form the best possible final version that will meet the goals and intentions of the producers.

A writer pens the story, a director coaches the actors, a cinematographer creates the visual style of each shot, and an editor puts all those pieces together. So an editor is really one of the last creative people to touch a motion picture project. It is his or her skill, craft, and gut instinct that help form the over-arching visual style of the presentation, and often it is also his or her choices that can make or break a program. Of course, an editor can only work as much magic as he or she is given, meaning that the initial quality and quantity of production footage has an awful lot to do with the overall appeal of the final, edited result. So certainly it is not all of the editor's responsibility when a project is well-received nor is it the editor's entire fault when things do not go well. But a good editor can make the difference in the overall final visual presentation.

This text, *Grammar of the Edit*, is designed to indoctrinate the beginner — the novice or the newbie — into the world of motion picture editing. The rules, guidelines, and general practices presented herein will hopefully provide a new student of this craft with a solid understanding of the basics and perhaps whet the appetite for further exploration of both the discipline's history and its trends toward tomorrow.

Regardless of which direction the fledgling editor will grow, everyone needs to learn how to walk before they can run and this text should help define the basic terms and clarify the common practices of editing. It does not mention specific computer-based video editing software or particular film-editing tools. It does not wish to delineate between images captured on motion picture emulsion film or on electronic analog or digital video mediums. The term "motion picture" may be used liberally to encompass a myriad of programming types whether shot for theaters, television, or the Web. A particular genre of film or a specific type of television programming may be called out in an example to help illustrate a unique point. The goal of this text is to inform a person new to editing about the most generic basics of accepted editing practices, the reasoning behind them, and their common interpreted meanings. Good technique and not so good technique may be discussed and illustrated, but in the end there is no right and there is no wrong, there is only what works and what does not work — and why.

Chapter One
Editing Basics

QUESTION: What is editing?

ANSWER: Editing for motion pictures is the process of organizing, reviewing, selecting, and assembling the picture and sound "footage" captured during production. The result of these editing efforts should be a coherent and meaningful story or visual presentation that comes as close as possible to achieving the goals behind the original intent of the work — to entertain, to inform, to inspire, etc.

When you write, you select words from your vocabulary and string them together in a particular fashion to construct sentences that will inform, entertain, or evoke emotional responses within the reader. When you edit a motion picture, there is a similar process. You have to select shots and string them together in edited scenes to inform, entertain, or evoke emotional responses within the viewer. For your written sentences to make sense to readers you must follow the known and accepted rules of grammar for your written language — spelling, word order, phrase structure, tense, etc. There is also a similar visual grammar for the language of motion pictures — how they are shot and how they are edited together.

In the companion text, *Grammar of the Shot*, these basic rules of structure and form in shooting the individual pictures are discussed in detail. This text, *Grammar of the Edit*, presents the basic rules of visual construction that will allow you to take these same shots and assemble them together into a meaningful story. As a creative entity, you may choose to edit your visual elements however you wish, but it must be understood that there are certain basic rules and guidelines that are commonly accepted in the entertainment and visual communication fields. The chapters of this book are designed to help you understand the grammar behind the editing process and set you on a path to good editing practices.

A Little Editing History

Long before the existence of digital videotape and computer editing software, people used emulsion film to create the illusion of motion pictures. Over one hundred years ago, the nascent technology of emulsion film strips and hand-cranked moving film cameras only allowed for roughly one minute of any event to be photographed. Many of the original movies were just roughly one-minute long recordings of events in real time. Very quickly the technologies advanced and the use of motion pictures moved from straight documentary presentations that amazed to more elaborate fictional narrative stories that entertained. Longer strips of film allowed for longer recording times. As film's visual language began to develop, more shot variety was introduced and motion pictures became grander in scope. Editing the larger amount of photographic material grew out of the need to trim the visual "fat" and to better structure the story shown to an audience.

Within just a short few decades, a more complex visual language of motion picture photography and editing had evolved. Films were quickly becoming the largest entertainment and information medium on the planet. They were held in high esteem by many and defamed by others. Motion pictures and how they were perceived by audiences became a source of study. Many theories about the impact of filmmaking, and the editing process especially, emerged from different cultures around the world.

When the editor cut the film and how the various shots were joined together were seen to have an impact on the viewing audience above and beyond the actual story. Editing was no longer just a means to physically trim the excess footage from a series of shots, but it had become recognized as a powerful tool in the filmmaker's toolbox. The machines used to take the pictures and to perform the cuts have evolved over time, but most of the basic rules of visual grammar have remained the same. Differing editorial styles have come and gone, but the core methods and intent behind the practice are unchanged even today.

What Factors May Impact Your Editing Choices?

So, if editing is the assembly of individual shots of picture and sound into a coherent story, then an **edit** must be the place where you transition from one of those shots into the next within that assembly. Put simply, an edit is a cut point — a place where one shot ends and another separate shot begins. (see Figure 1.2) The term "cut" stems from the days when motion pictures were shot and edited on very long strips of emulsion film. Looking at the individual still frames on that strip of film, the editor would determine where to physically cut the film between pictures. A pair of scissors or a razor blade device was used to actually cut the film at that point (see Figure 1.1). Glue or tape was then used to join the different cut strips of plastic film together again. The cut or join then becomes the point of transition from one shot to the next. The straight cut described here is just one way to move between shots. How you choose to transition from one shot to another depends on many variables.

The first factor you may wish to consider is what medium you are using to perform the physical edits — film, tape-to-tape video, or computer-aided digital video. Each medium, and the devices that are used in the editing process, can often dictate physical, time-related, or financial limitations. Many argue that computer-aided digital video editing is the most economical and the most diverse as far as options for editing go, and it is, most likely, the type of editing that you, the reader, will be performing. In this text we are attempting to keep the discussions of editing grammar as generic as possible, so the general rules and practices presented should apply to any medium and to any editing device or software. Just be aware that certain terminology used in one medium may have its origins rooted in another and may vary from one software application to another.

A second factor that may impact your editing transition choices can be the kind of project that you are editing. Are you assembling footage for a documentary, a fictional narrative short film, a news package, a music video, a television commercial, or a cousin's

FIGURE 1.1 Initially, editing motion picture film required very basic technologies.

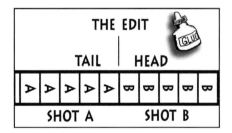

FIGURE 1.2 The film strip of shot B is "edited" onto the end of shot A.

wedding video? Each type of project or program may necessitate a certain editing style and usage of particular transitions. For instance, you may wish to use long, slow dissolves from one shot to the next in a moody music video, but you would never consider using long, slow dissolves in a hard-hitting, factual news package for the six o'clock news. We will discuss dissolves in more detail later, but the example illustrates the importance of following the accepted rules and guidelines of style for differing program types and for genres within those distinct types. For the purposes of clarity and simplicity, we will mostly focus on the grammar and practices associated with fictional narrative motion picture storytelling, but the general guidelines apply to all forms of motion image programming.

Other factors involved with editorial and transition choices include your own creativity, the vision of the director, the suggestions of a producer, and the quality of the raw footage that you are tasked with editing together. Remember, the right editor can breathe new life into old, tired, or boring material, but an editor may still have to answer to other limiting factors as discussed above. The point is, an editor performs the task of editing but she or he does not always have control over the many variables that impact the process.

What Factors May Impact Your Editing Choices?

The Basic Edit Transitions

Let us begin our discussion of editing with the edit point itself.

There are four basic ways one can transition from one shot or visual element into another:

- **Cut** — An instantaneous change from one shot to the next. The last full frame of picture for one shot is immediately followed by the first full frame of picture for the next shot.
- **Dissolve** — A gradual change from the ending pictures of one shot into the beginning pictures of the next shot. This is traditionally achieved via a superimposition of both shots with a simultaneous downward and upward ramping of opacity over a particular period of time. As the end of the first shot "dissolves" away, the beginning of the next shot "resolves" onto the screen at the same time.
- **Wipe** — A line, progressing at some angle, or a shape, moves across the screen removing the image of the shot just ending while simultaneously revealing the next shot behind the line or the shape. The wiping shot replaces the previous shot on the screen.
- **Fade** — (1) A gradual change from a solid black screen into a fully visible image (fade from black or fade-in). (2) A gradual change from a fully visible image into a solid black screen (fade to black or fade-out).

The grammar of the edit has evolved in some ways since the early days of cinema, but these four basic transitions have remained the same. No matter what type of program you are editing or what tool you are using to make it, a cut is still a cut. A dissolve is still a dissolve no matter what pictures you dissolve from and to. A wipe will literally wipe a new shot over the old shot. A fade-in still comes out of black and a fade-out still goes into black. They have remained the same because their individual purposes have remained the same, and, for the most part, everyone around the world understands their grammar — or what it means when they see one being used as a transition.

Later in this text you will be able to explore a more in-depth analysis of these basic editing transitions. For now, let us place them aside and focus our attentions on a much broader topic — a general approach to the entire editing process.

Your goal is to have a finished piece that plays for your audience and provides as much entertainment or information as it can. To achieve that finished piece, though, there are several stages of the editing process that you will, most likely, need to follow.

Stages of the Editing Process

The editing process, more generally referred to as **post-production** or sometimes just **post**, can range from being rather simple to extremely complex. The post-production period really encompasses any and all work on the project that comes after the shooting (the **production**) is completed. Picture and sound tracks are edited together to show and tell the story, special visual effects are generated, titles/graphics/credits are added, sound effects are created, and music is scored during post-production. On smaller projects, one person can do all of this work, but on larger productions, several teams of women and men work in various departments to complete each element and join each phase of the post-production workflow.

The following is a low-level listing of the major steps involved in a post-production workflow that stresses the editing process for the visual elements of a project.

- Acquire
- Organize
- Review and select
- Assemble
- Cut — rough
- Cut — fine
- Picture lock
- Master and deliver

Acquisition — Simply put, you must acquire the footage shot by the production team. Motion picture and sound elements, whether on emulsion film, analog tape, digital tape, or digital files, must be gathered together for the duration of the post-production editing process. The medium of choice depends on the method of editing and the physical devices used to perform the edits. If you are using a computer-aided digital non-linear editing system to perform the edit, then you will have to import, capture, or "digitize" all materials as media on your storage drives. These media files must remain accessible by your editing software for the life of the project for you to complete the work.

Organization — All of the minutes, hours, feet, reels, or gigabytes of picture and sound elements should be organized in some way. If you do not have a clear system of labeling, grouping, or sorting all of the material needed for your project, you will eventually have a difficult time finding that good shot or that good sound effect, etc. Organization of source materials is not the most glamorous part of the edit process, but it can certainly make the difference between a smooth post-production workflow and a slower and more frustrating one. Many of the better editors and **assistant editors** are highly prized for their organizational skills. Tame the chaos into order and craft the order into a motion picture.

Review and selection — Once you have acquired and organized all of your elements, it will be necessary to review all of this material and pick out the best pieces that will work for your project. You will "pull the selects" and set aside the good stuff while weeding out the junk that you hope you will not have to use. You would be wise to not actually throw anything away, however, because you will never know what might come in handy a day or a few weeks into the editing process. That one scrap of footage of the flag waving in the breeze may just save the entire edit, so keep it readily available even though you know it is not one of your original selections.

Assembly — This process calls for assembling all of the major pieces of the project into a logical **sequence** of picture and sound elements. If you are editing a scripted story, you would follow that script as a blueprint for assembling the best selections of the various shots of the scenes that make up the motion picture. If you are creating a documentary or even a music video, there is always some story that is trying to be shown to an audience — assemble those raw parts into this skeleton version. No matter what genre the project, the story, in its longest and most rough-hewn form, takes shape now.

Rough cut — This is a stage of the project's development where the majority of the "fat" has been trimmed and you are left with a presentation that is complete in its narrative flow but has many rough edges. Perhaps not every cut is perfectly timed yet, there are no finalized titles or graphics, simple or more elaborate effects have not been created, and the audio mix certainly has not been completed. You do have the timing of the main elements down to a good pace, however, and you, and others to whom you show the developing work, like how the story unfolds, although restructuring of scenes may still occur.

Fine cut — You have worked and re-worked and massaged the material of your project into a tight and finely tuned presentation. There will be no major renovations from this point forward. You, and the majority of the people to whom you show the piece, all agree that no further tweaks are required. This cut is fine.

Picture lock — You have reached picture lock when you are absolutely certain that you will not make any more changes to the picture track(s) of your edited piece.

The timing of all picture elements (shots, titles, black pauses, etc.) is set. Once you have locked the picture tracks (sometimes literally but mostly figuratively), you are then free to address your audio mixing needs. Once the audio tweaks are finalized and your music is in place, then you are ready for the last stage.

Mastering and delivery — All of your efforts in creating a well-edited piece will mean very little if you cannot deliver the show to the audience that needs to see it. These days this process may mean recording your final cut onto videotape, creating an optical film print for projection in a movie theatre, converting

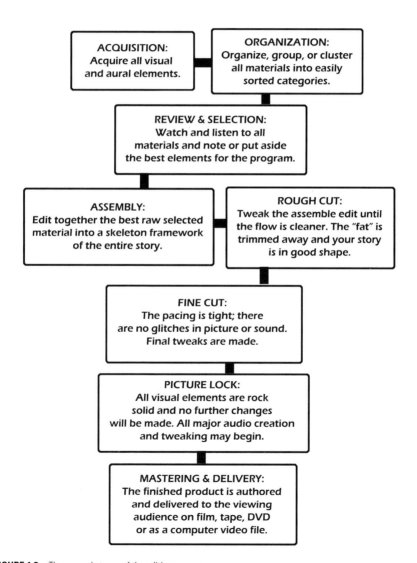

Stages of the Editing Process

FIGURE 1.3   The general stages of the editing process.

your story into a computer video file, or authoring the piece onto a DVD. Each medium would require a unique process, but the end result is that you have a fully mastered version of your show and an audience gets to view all of your hard editing work.

So we now have a pretty good idea of what the basic editing, or post-production work-flow is for any project large or small. You certainly may encounter projects that do not call for all the stages of editing to be executed in a clearly delineated manner, but, for the most part, you will touch upon some combination of each of these stages as you work toward your finished piece.

End of Chapter One Review

1. There are basic and widely accepted rules of visual grammar that govern the motion picture editing process.

2. The grammar of the edit has evolved over a century of filmmaking, but the basics, covered in this book, have remained largely unchanged.

3. There are many factors that play a role in how a motion picture is edited and the editor does not always have control over many of them.

4. The four basic types of transition edits are cut, dissolve, wipe, and fade.

5. The basic post-production workflow consists of the following stages: acquisition, organization, review and selection, assembly, rough cut, fine cut, picture lock, and master and delivery.

Chapter Two
Understanding the Footage

QUESTION: Why should an editor be well versed in the various shot types?

ANSWER: Consider the individual shot types as the vocabulary — the visual phrases — used to edit together complete scenes in a motion picture. Knowing the "words" and their meaning will help an editor construct more meaningful visual sentences.

When you watch a stage play, a music concert, or a sports event in an actual public theatre, club, or stadium you generally only get to observe the actions of the performers from one static viewpoint — your seat. If any of these events were recorded and broadcast on television, the person watching at home, although missing out on the thrill of being at the live event, will benefit from having a more "intimate" viewing experience thanks to the event's coverage by multiple cameras of varying positions and lens focal lengths. The person at home "sees" more views and details than the person at the actual event.

It is this same concept of coverage that allows people watching a motion picture to feel as though they are observing actual events unfolding before their eyes. They get to "see" more because the camera records the people, places, and actions from many different vantage points and with varying degrees of detail. The production team photographs all of the important action from what they consider to be the most advantageous and necessary points of view. Each one of these camera views is called a shot.

These shots, or individual units of visual information, are eventually given to the editor during post-production. Even though the editor had no control over which shots were recorded on the film set or how they were composed, it will be his or her job to review all of the material and choose the best viewpoints — pull the selects — and combine these various shots to show the audience the best visual presentation of the action in the story, whatever it may be.

Basic Shot Types

Most editors only get involved with a project during post-production. Although many professional editors may have worked in production on a film set or in a studio at some point in their careers, it is not that common for them to work both production and post-production jobs. What is common, however, is the need for all editors to know certain production concepts and terminologies and be well-versed in the visual grammar of filmmaking. Knowing the basic shot types and how to best juxtapose them during the edit is a key responsibility for the editor. He or she must know how to best "show" the story. So as a review, we will present the following section which highlights and illustrates the main building blocks of film language — the basic shots.

- Extreme close-up (XCU or ECU)
- Big close-up (BCU)
- Close-up (CU)
- Medium close-up (MCU)
- Medium shot (MS)
- Medium long shot (MLS)
- Long shot (LS) or wide shot (WS)
- Very long shot (VLS)
- Extreme long shot (XLS or ELS)
- Two shot (2S)
- Over the shoulder (OTS)

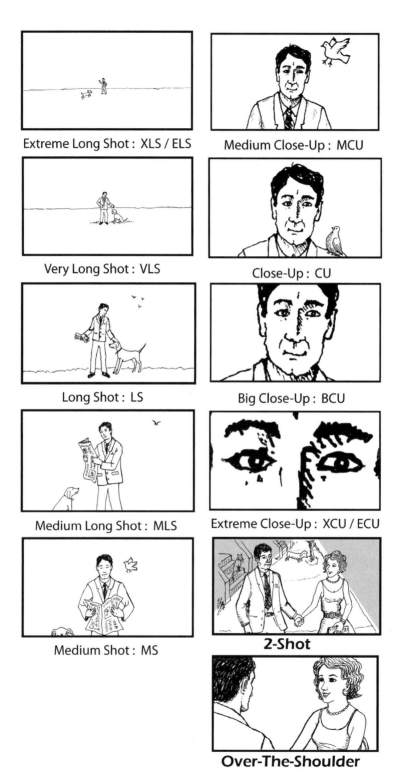

Extreme Long Shot : XLS / ELS

Medium Close-Up : MCU

Very Long Shot : VLS

Close-Up : CU

Long Shot : LS

Big Close-Up : BCU

Medium Long Shot : MLS

Extreme Close-Up : XCU / ECU

Medium Shot : MS

2-Shot

Over-The-Shoulder

FIGURE 2.1 The extended family of film's basic shot types.

Shot Descriptions

The basic shot types can be used to record any subject or objects of varying sizes, but to keep the examples grounded in an easily understood relationship, we are going to mainly focus our attention on the framing of a human subject. It should then be pretty clear, based on the following shot descriptions, how to create similar framing when recording objects or **film space** devoid of human figures.

Extreme Close-Up (XCU or ECU)

1. Purely a detail shot. The framing favors one aspect of a subject such as his or her eyes, mouth, ear, or hand; may be a magnification of any object or item or merely just a part of an object or item.

2. Lacking any points of reference to the surrounding environment, the audience has no context in which to place this body part or object detail, so understanding will stem from how or when this shot is edited into the motion picture. It is often helpful, but not required, that the subject whose body detail is displayed in the XCU is shown before or after in a wider shot so context may be established for the viewer.

3. This type of extremely magnified imagery can be used in documentary work such as medical films or scientific studies, more fanciful projects like music videos and experimental art films, or it may be used sparingly in a fictional narrative story.

FIGURE 2.2   Examples of extreme close-up (XCU/ECU) shots.

Big Close-Up (BCU)

1. Human face occupies as much of the frame as possible and still shows the key features of eyes, nose, and mouth at once.

2. Such an intimate shot puts the audience directly in the face of the subject. Every detail of the face is highly visible, therefore facial movements or expressions need to be subtle. Very little head movement can be tolerated before the subject moves out of frame.

3. This shot is about who and how that "who" feels — angry, scared, romantic, etc.

Close-Up (CU)

1. Sometimes called a "head shot" because the framing is primarily the face, but it may cut off the top of the subject's hair. The bottom of frame can begin anywhere just below the chin or with the neck and a little upper shoulder visible.

2. A very intimate full face shot of a human subject showing all detail in the eyes. It conveys the subtle emotions that play across the eyes, mouth, and facial muscles of an actor. Health conditions and facial hair in men and make-up use in women are clearly visible.

3. An audience member should be totally focused on the human face with this framing.

4. This shot shows who but not so much where or when.

FIGURE 2.3 Examples of big close-up (BCU) shots.

FIGURE 2.4   Examples of close-up (CU) shots.

FIGURE 2.5   Examples of medium close-up (MCU) shots.

Medium Close-Up (MCU)

1. Sometimes called a "two-button" for the tight bottom frame cutting off at the chest, roughly where you would see the top two buttons on a shirt. Definitely cuts off above the elbow joint. Adjust bottom frame slightly for men or women depending on costuming.

2. Character's facial features are rather clear. Where the eyes look is obvious, as is emotion, hair style and color, make-up, etc. This is one of the most common shots in filmmaking because it provides so much information about the character while speaking, listening, or performing an action that does not involve much body or head movement.

3. An audience is supposed to be watching the human face at this point in the framing so actions or objects in the surrounding environment should hold little to no importance.

4. Depending upon general lighting and costuming you may discern general information about where and when.

Medium Shot (MS)

1. May also be called the "waist" shot because the frame cuts off the human figure just below the waist and just above the wrists if arms are down at the side.

FIGURE 2.6 Examples of medium shots (MS).

FIGURE 2.7 Examples of medium long shots (MLS).

2. Human torso is most prominent in the frame. However, eyes and the direction they look, clothing, and hair color and style are all plainly visible.

3. Subject movement may become a concern since the tighter framing restricts the freedom of gesture. Be careful not to **break frame** (have an actor's body part touch or move beyond the established edge of the picture frame).

4. Certainly shows who and may provide generic detail about where (inside or outside, apartment, store, forest, etc.) and when (day or night, season).

Medium Long Shot (MLS)

1. First shot where surrounding environment occupies more screen space than the subject. Traditionally framed such that bottom of frame cuts off the leg either just below, or, more common, just above the knee. The choice for where to frame the leg may depend on costuming or body movement of the individual in the shot. If you cut bottom of frame above the knee, it is sometimes referred to as the "cowboy." (In classical Hollywood Westerns, it was important to get the obligatory "six gun" strapped to the hero's thigh in the shot.)

2. Human figure is prominent and details in clothing, gender, and facial expressions are visible.

3. Shows more of who than where and may still show when.

Long Shot/Wide Shot (LS/WS)

1. This is usually considered a "full body" shot, wide but still in close to the figure often framing feet just above bottom of frame and head just below top of frame. It may often be noted as a generic wide shot (WS) as well.

2. The tall vertical line of the human figure attracts the viewer's eye away from the surrounding environment; however, a fair amount of the character's surroundings are still visible and should be considered in the composition.

3. May not work well for an **establishing shot** because it may not show enough of the environment to provide the required information to the audience.

4. Shows where, when, and who. The gender, clothing, movements, and general facial expressions may be seen but real facial detail is lacking.

Very Long Shot (VLS)

1. Proud member of the wide shot family.

2. May be used in **exterior** or **interior** shooting when enough width and height exist within the studio set or location building.

3. The human figure is visible but only generalities of race, mood, clothing, and hair may be observed. The environment within the film space dominates much of the screen.

4. May be used as an establishing shot where movement of character brings the figure closer to the camera during the action of the shot.

5. Shows where, when, and a bit of who.

FIGURE 2.8 Examples of long shots (LS).

Extreme Long Shot (XLS/ELS)

1. Also referred to as a very wide shot or a very wide angle shot.

2. Traditionally used in exterior shooting.

3. Encompasses a large field of view, therefore forms an image that shows a large amount of the environment within the film space.

4. Often used as an establishing shot at the beginning of a motion picture or at the start of a new sequence within a motion picture.

5. Shows urban, suburban, rural, mountains, desert, ocean, etc.

6. May show day, night, summer, winter, spring, fall, distant past, past, present, future, etc.

7. May show the lone stranger walking into town or massive invading army. Most often the human figures in the XLS are so small that details are indistinguishable. General, not specific information will be conveyed.

FIGURE 2.9 Examples of very long shots (VLS).

FIGURE 2.10 Examples of extreme long shots (ELS/XLS).

Shot Descriptions

Two-Shot (2-Shot/2S)

1. Contains two subjects who generally either face toward camera or face each other in profile to camera.

2. Framing depends on whether the subjects are standing or sitting, moving or static, or making gestures and performing actions. A medium 2-shot (M2S) is common but allows for little gesturing or body movement. Medium long shot or long shot two-shots will allow more room around the subjects for movement or action.

3. Framing for tighter shots (MCU, CU) would entail extremely close proximity of subjects' heads implying intimate connectivity or aggressive posturing like two boxers in a clutch. To see both faces of the subjects in a tight 2-shot, you would have to "favor" one body before the other, literally overlapping the people within the frame. The person closest to camera and seen fully by the viewer is given favor.

4. Adding persons creates a three-shot (3-shot), a group shot, or a crowd shot depending on how many individuals are clustered together in the frame.

FIGURE 2.11 The 2-shot, the overlapping 2S, and the group shot.

Over-the-Shoulder Shot (OTS/OSS)

1. A special 2-shot in which one subject is "favored" facing camera either frame left or frame right and the other subject has his or her back turned toward camera on the opposite side of the frame. The non-favored subject creates an "L" shape at the edge and bottom of frame with the back of their head and their shoulder; hence the name. The camera shoots over one subject's shoulder to frame up the face of the other subject for the viewer to see.

2. Due to the "shoulder" subject partially cut off at the edge of frame, the shot type used for the OTS may be as tight as a medium close-up. Anything closer and the composition would alter the balance of the frame and the shoulder may get lost creating what some may call a **dirty single**.

3. It is often helpful to have a decreased **depth of field** so the portion of the "shoulder" subject visible in the corner of the frame is blurry while the face of the favored subject is well-focused. Having a well-focused back-of-the-head may prove to be distracting for the audience.

FIGURE 2.12 Examples of over-the-shoulder (OTS) framing.

Increasing Shot Complexity

It is worth noting that all of the shot types outlined above have one thing in common: they belong to an over-arching shot category that we like to call simple shots. They could, however, evolve into two more of our categories — complex shots or developing shots. Before we clarify what constitutes a simple, complex, or developing shot, we should give just a bit of attention to the four basic elements of shot creation whose presence helps dictate into which category a shot may be placed.

LENS — Does the camera's lens move during the shot? Does the lens alter its light gathering characteristics while the shot is being recorded? Since the camera is stationary, lens movement can only be achieved while using a **zoom** or a **vari-focal** lens. So you have to determine if there is a zoom or a **focal length** change during the shot.

CAMERA — Does the entire camera body move during the shot? Essentially, is there a panning action or a tilting action executed while the camera is recording the shot? The camera mount (**tripod head**) would have to allow for these horizontal and vertical axis changes, but the camera support (**tripod**) would not be in motion.

MOUNT/SUPPORT — Does the camera's mount or support physically move the camera around the film set or location during a shot? In a television studio the camera is mounted atop a **pedestal,** which can boom up (raise camera height) or boom down (lower camera height) and roll around the smooth floor. On a film set, the camera can be mounted to a moving **dolly** on tracks (for **crab** or **truck** moves), it can be attached to a **crane** or **jib arm**, or suspended from cables or a Steadicam and so forth.

SUBJECT — Does the subject recorded with the camera move during the shot? The subject can be a person or multiple people, an animal, an animate object (something capable of moving itself like a remote-controlled toy car), or an inanimate object (something that does not move, like a vase or a pirate's treasure chest).

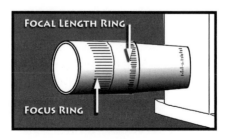

FIGURE 2.13　A camera lens with zoom or vari-focal capabilities.

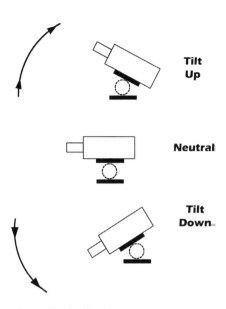

FIGURE 2.14 Camera mounted to pan/tilt tripod head.

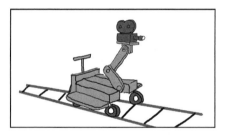

FIGURE 2.15 A camera on a dolly.

FIGURE 2.16 Subjects in motion and at rest.

As the editor, you will not have to consciously analyze each shot you are given for these four elements. Most often their presence or lack thereof will be rather noticeable. What you should understand though are the basic categories that shots will fall into when one or several of the four elements are present. These three basic categories are **simple shots**, **complex shots**, and **developing shots**. Defining these over-arching shot categories now will help us in our analysis of editing them together — a topic we cover later in this text.

Increasing Shot Complexity

Simple Shots

- No lens movement
- No camera movement
- No mount movement
- Simple subject movement

Simple shots are just that — simple. They have no focal length changes (zooms). They have no tilting or panning actions. They show no camera body movement as with a dolly or a jib. They do show the subject move in simple ways across screen, standing, sitting, etc. The basic shot types, discussed earlier, are all covered from a particular angle, with a set focal length on the lens and a **locked-off** mount. Whatever simple action unfolds before the camera, it happens within that set and finite framing. Often, simple shots can make up the bulk of fictional narrative dialogue driven motion picture content.

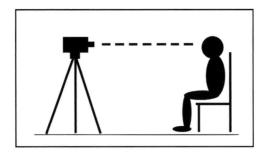

FIGURE 2.17   Simple shot with no lens, camera, or mounting movement but maybe talent movement.

Complex Shots

- Lens movement
- Camera movement
- No mount movement
- Simple subject movement

A complex shot may contain a:

- Pan
- Tilt
- Pan and tilt (diagonal upward or downward camera lens movement)
- Lens movement (zoom or a focus pull)
- Lens movement and a pan (hiding a zoom by panning the camera)
- Lens movement and a tilt (hiding the zoom by tilting the camera)
- Subject movement and a pan
- Subject movement and a tilt

So if a shot contains any combination of the three active elements (lens movement, camera movement, or simple subject movement), then it may be considered a complex shot.

If the complex shot does contain a **pan** or a **tilt** then the production team should have ensured that it begins with a static start frame, goes through its move, and completes with a static end frame. The static start and end frames of these pan and tilt shots are very important to the editor. You will find that it is very difficult to cut from a static shot into a shot already in motion, or cut out of a motion shot to a static shot. Entering or leaving movement at the cut can be very jarring for an audience. The best case scenario is for you to be presented with pan and tilt shots that start and end with static frames and contain smooth even movement in between.

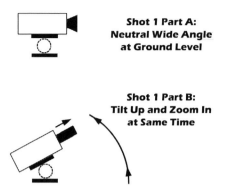

Shot 1 Part A:
Neutral Wide Angle
at Ground Level

Shot 1 Part B:
Tilt Up and Zoom In
at Same Time

FIGURE 2.18   A complex shot can combine a zoom with a camera tilt and subject movement.

Developing Shots

- Lens movement
- Camera movement
- Mounting movement
- More complex subject movement

A developing shot incorporates movement on all four elements. As such, you can imagine that these shots are rather difficult to accomplish. As subjects move in complicated blocking patterns on set, the camera is moved about on a mount (perhaps a dolly or a crane boom arm), the lens is being re-focused or perhaps zoomed, and there will be a panning or tilting action at some point to follow the action.

As an editor, you should watch these developing shots very carefully for quality assurance. They will most likely start and end with static frames, but the middle portion could be a grab-bag of actions. Watch for proper focus, good framing, and smooth movements. Since these types of elaborate developing shots are designed by the filmmakers to be used as one stunning show piece, there is often little actual editing that you may need to do beyond cutting the shot into the overall scene at the appropriate point. Cutting into and out of moving developing shots can upset the flow of the entire shot and take away from its impact on the viewing audience. This may be necessary, however, for creative purposes or if some of the action within the developing shot is not top quality.

FIGURE 2.19　A developing shot follows complex action with lens, camera, and mounting movement.

Reviewing the Footage — Selecting the Best Shots

We should all feel rather comfortable now identifying the various types of shots that may be used to record the images of a motion picture. With these committed to memory, it will be that much easier to organize them when you acquire and review the footage to be edited. Be forewarned, however, that not every shot type may be used to generate coverage for a particular scene. For example, looking for an XLS in footage from an airplane cockpit dialogue scene may not make much sense.

Once you have the material organized, it will be helpful to review each shot for its technical and aesthetic qualities. Certain criteria work for some motion picture genres but not all movies, programs, commercials, or music videos can be held up to one master checklist of good or bad qualities. What might never be allowed as acceptable in one program type may be entirely encouraged in another. So, as an editor, you will have to make your own judgment calls depending on the type of project you are editing and what the end goals of that project are set to be.

What Could Make or Break a Shot?

The listing that follows, although certainly not exhaustive, should provide plenty of criteria upon which you might base an analysis of the footage you will be editing. Again, the type of show you have to cut will often come with its own style, traditions, and sense of what is acceptable and what is not, but you should always be aware of these potential "gotchas."

- Focus
- Audio quality
- Exposure and color temperature
- Framing and composition
- Screen direction
- 180 degree rule
- 30 degree rule
- Matching angles
- Matching eye-line
- Continuity of action
- Continuity of dialogue
- Performance

Focus

One of the chief issues that you may encounter as an editor is incorrect focus during a
shot. Nothing can ruin a good performance like bad focus. It is the camera department's
job to ensure good focus on shots, and, for the most part, they do excellent work. It only
takes one false move or late start with the focus pull to turn a potentially good take
into a bad one. With scripted fictional narrative filmmaking, the production team will
often shoot multiple takes of a line reading or an action to ensure that they have the
focus correct, so you should not have to worry too much with that material. Unscripted
projects, like documentaries, corporate interview videos, or live news often only have
one chance at good focus while the action happens in front of the camera. A soft focus
talking head interview could render that entire interview unusable.

Why is soft focus or blurry imagery so bad? It is the one technical factor in film or video
that cannot be corrected during post-production. Unlike exposure, color correctness, or
even framing, there is no fix for soft focus footage. It becomes a problem because the
viewing audience is intolerant of blurry images. As humans, our visual system is set to
always see things in sharp focus (unless, of course, you require glasses or other correc-
tive lenses to properly focus the light in your eyes). When we watch a moving image
that has soft focus, we become distracted and uncomfortable as our eyes try to focus
on the screen image that cannot resolve. It is unnatural for us to see things blurry, so
when a filmmaker purposefully causes things to go blurry in a shot, it must be quickly
followed by placing some object within the frame in good focus as soon as possible.
So unless you are experimenting with radical focus shifts while shooting footage for a
music video, you should not be using blurry takes when you edit.

FIGURE 2.20   Audiences may forgive many things about an image, but they do not tolerate blurry pictures. Use the shots that have the best focus.

Focus

Audio Quality

Another big technical issue with footage for a project will be poor audio quality. The synchronized sound, whether from a two-system film shoot or a single-system video shoot, must be of good quality to use it in the final **audio mix**. Unlike bad focus, there are some tricks that can be done to improve the sound quality of the audio, mostly achieved with computer software these days. If the audio is really bad and cannot be salvaged by tweaking with an audio software package, then you still have the option of replacing it all together with new, cleanly recorded audio to match the picture exactly. Some refer to this as **looping** or **automatic dialogue replacement** (ADR). So if the pictures are good, but the audio is bad, depending on the project, time, and money, the footage may still be usable.

FIGURE 2.21   Choose material with the best audio first, but there may be ways to do a simple fix with audio "sweetening" software.

Audio Quality

Exposure and Color Temperature

With the advent of more powerful video editing software, issues with the **exposure and color temperature** of the footage are no longer that difficult to fix. Of course, you would prefer that all shots were well-exposed and had the proper look for the color palette from the very beginning, so you really should start by selecting those first. But, if good material is present on shots that have exposure issues (overall image is too bright or too dark) or color temperature shifts (image looking overly blue or overly orange, etc.), then keep those shots for use and have yourself or a video technician attend to their corrections with the software tools available. If you have no tools for such a purpose, then look for other properly exposed and color-balanced footage to use.

Audiences struggle with imagery that is either too bright or too dark, and they do not like it if someone has green skin when there is no reason in the story for them to have green skin. Additionally, consider your own editing needs. How would it look to cut back and forth from a dark shot to a very bright shot. Our eyes would be missing valuable screen imagery and possible audio information as our brains adjust our eyes between the extremes of dark and light. Without getting too technical, these types of sudden exposure extremes can also cause image quality issues with video playback on computer and television screens. For everyone's sake, either correct the exposure or color issues or do not use the footage in the final project if at all possible.

FIGURE 2.22 Select the well-exposed shots. If you have to edit using dark or light shots, most video editing software packages come with some built-in exposure and color correcting tools to help.

Framing and Composition

Living at the cusp between a technical issue and an aesthetic issue is the framing of a shot. It can be considered technical in the sense that sometimes the format of the recording device (film or video camera) may be larger than the frame size for the final deliverable product. This is especially true these days when people shooting wide screen **16:9 high definition** (**HD**) may be looking to finish the show at a traditional aspect ratio of **4:3** for **standard definition** (**SD**) television. As an editor, you may be called upon to **reformat** the video frame (cut it down to a smaller size for TV or the Web), or perform what is called a **pan and scan**, where you take a wide screen camera original format and extract a smaller frame size from it while simultaneously panning left and right to maintain some semblance of good composition in the new, smaller image.

Aesthetic criteria for framing and composition have fewer immediate fixes. You will have to watch complex and developing shots for good focus, but also for good framing and proper composition. If an elaborate camera move bumps, jumps, sways, or in some way misses its mark while covering talent or action, then you should not consider using that particular take, or at least not that particular portion of that take. Again, during production, there are normally quality controls for reviewing each shot, and if they do not get it right they usually perform the shot again, so you should have at least one good choice for your edit, but not always. That is where creative cutting comes into play.

Of course, you will also wish to gauge the qualitative attributes of a shot. Is there appropriate **head room**? Is there appropriate **look room** or **looking room**? Is the **horizon line** parallel to the top and bottom edges of the frame (if it should be)? Is the vertical **camera angle** too high or too low? Is the horizontal camera angle too **subjective** or too **objective**? Does it work with the type of project you are editing? Very few of these other aesthetic shot qualities can be fixed by the editor (short of using some software effects to resize or rotate an image) so it might be best to place them on the back burner and use any other better takes.

FIGURE 2.23   (A–B) An example of an SDTV 4:3 extraction from an HDTV 16:9 widescreen image. (C) An example of a frame with good head room, look room, and a visible horizon line. (D–E) High and low angles on a subject. (F–G) Examples of subjective camera coverage and objective shooting style.

Framing and Composition

Screen Direction

This is mostly an issue with scripted fictional narrative footage, but it comes up in other genres as well. Talent or subject movement out of the frame of one shot and into the frame of another shot must maintain consistent screen direction. To clarify, frame left is screen left and frame right is screen right when watching the images. The film space itself, the world in which the characters live and move, must be considered as real space; therefore it is subject to the same rules of left, right, up, down, etc.

If shot A shows a character exiting frame left of a simple shot, then when you cut to shot B, the same character must be entering from frame right. The character's direction of movement within the film space must be consistent — right to left and right to left again. If you show a character exiting frame left in shot A, then show the same character entering from frame left in shot B, it will appear as though the character has simply turned around but is magically re-entering a different location. This will confuse your viewing audience and cause them to mentally recoil against the edit.

FIGURE 2.24   Maintaining screen direction of talent movement between shots helps orient the viewer within the film space.

180 Degree Rule/Axis of Action

Continuing the logic of our **screen direction** discussion, you must also analyze the footage to make sure that the production team respected the **axis of action** or the **imaginary line** while they were shooting coverage for the various scenes. As a quick review, the 180 degree rule is established from the first camera set up covering the action of a scene, which is usually a wide shot showing the players and the environment. An imaginary line, following the direction of the talent's **sight line**, cuts across the set or location and it defines what is frame left and what is frame right. Each successive medium or close-up shot of the talent within the scene must all be set up on the same side of this **line of action** or else, to the viewing audience, the spatial relationships of the talent will be flipped left to right or right to left. Screen direction is maintained by shooting all the coverage from the one side of this line.

If you consider one of the alternate names for this practice, the **180 degree rule**, it might help clarify what is going on. When the camera crew photographs a two-person dialogue scene for the wide long shot, they have established the side of the room from which they will continue to shoot for the other, closer shots they will need for coverage. If you imagine a circle running around the central talent, then the camera can only operate within one-half of that full circle, or within a 180 degree arc. The imaginary line has bisected the full circle and made a semi-circle within which the camera can move for more shooting. Should the camera have been moved across the line to shoot an individual's close-up, that character, once edited into the scene, will appear to be turning and facing the opposite direction. This will look incorrect to the audience because the anomalous shot will break from the established screen directions for this scene. As a result, you really cannot edit in a shot that has **crossed the line**.

FIGURE 2.25 Coverage shots that "cross the line" are generally not usable because they break the established screen direction for the scene.

30 Degree Rule

Based around the concept of the 180 degree rule, the **30 degree rule** calls for the camera crew to move the camera around the 180 degree arc by at least 30 degrees before they set up for a new coverage shot of talent. The reason is simple. If two shots, say a medium long shot and a medium shot, of one person are shot from two locations around the 180 degree arc and the physical distance between camera set-ups is less than 30 degrees, then the two shots, when cut together by the editor, will look too similar and cause a "jump" in the mind of the viewer.

This is where the expression **jump cut** comes from. Without sufficient movement around the shooting arc, the viewpoint that the camera offers is too similar. If you have to edit these two similar shots together, the imagery will appear to suffer an immediate jump in space and possibly in time. The angles of coverage and the shot type must be different enough to allow a believable alteration in view points across the cut. As the editor, you cannot control where the camera was placed for the close-up coverage, but you do have control over what two shots you juxtapose together at a cut point, provided there are more than two angles of coverage. Make sure that the two shots are sufficiently different enough in **angle on action** so they do not appear to "jump" while viewing them together.

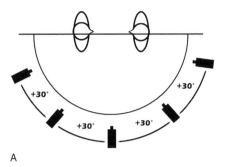

FIGURE 2.26 It is best to edit coverage shots whose individual angles on action are greater than 30 degrees apart along the 180 degree arc. If the camera angles covering the action are too similar, as in this example, the audience will perceive the edit as a jump cut.

30 Degree Rule

Matching Angles

When shooting dialogue scenes, the production team will most often shoot what are called **matching angles** — coverage of each character in each shot type where the angle on the person, their size in the frame, and the focus on their face are all consistent with one another. One person's close-up will look very similar to the other person's close-up, but they will be on opposite sides of the frame. As an editor, you will often like to cut from one person's shot (whatever shot type it may be) to the other person's matching shot. The back and forth imagery will be easily accepted by the viewing audience because the images, although of two different people on opposite sides of the screen, look like they belong together. In other words, they match.

FIGURE 2.27   Use matching angles for shot types when editing coverage for a scene involving more than one person.

Matching Eye-Line

Eye-line (sight line) is an imaginary line that connects a character's eyes to whatever object holds his or her attention within the film world. If two people are speaking with one another, the other person's face or eyes are often the object of interest, so the eye-line would **trace** from character A's eyes to character B's face/eyes. It could be a person looking at a wall clock, or a dog, or a pile of money. The tricky part arises when you are editing closer shots of people and the object of interest (the thing looked at) is not in the same frame. When you cut the shot of the person next to the shot of the object of interest, the eye-line must match (see Figure 2.28). An audience member must be able to trace the imaginary line from the eyes to the object across the cut point and into the new shot. If this line does not flow correctly, then the audience will feel like something is just not right. As an editor, you cannot really fix eye-line mistakes; you will just have to find some other way to cut around the issue (see the use of **cut-away** shots later in the text).

FIGURE 2.28   The eye-line or imaginary lines of attention should match across the transition between two shots.

Matching Eye-line

Continuity of Action

We will discuss this in greater detail later in the book, but it is a topic that frustrates many editors. The action performed by or around the talent in one shot must match, relatively exactly, the same action performed in a different angle within the same scene. Humans are very good about determining fluidity of motion. When things do not flow — when supposedly continuous actions do not match across a cut point — it is easily noticed (see Figure 2.29). Your job will be to finesse these action cuts as best as possible. Unless there is an obvious glitch in one entire shot, you may not be able to tell that action is not matching until after the footage review stage. Save all the good takes and see which ones eventually cut best with one another.

FIGURE 2.29   Be watchful of continuity issues within the shots you are considering for the edit. Here, the coffee mug jumps hands across the cut point.

Continuity of Dialogue

Be aware of line delivery when reviewing the footage. Does the talent say different words from take to take and shot to shot? Is there a different timbre in the voice or a modified rate of delivery? Some of these issues may be cut around by laying in different audio from alternate takes and so forth, but sometimes things just will not match. As with most audio issues, there may be a way around them for a fix, so keep the footage for later use, but try to separate out all the best and most usable takes first.

Dialogue: "I said no sugar."

Dialogue: "I said no cream."

FIGURE 2.30   Lines of dialogue that stray from the script may still be used or even replaced.

Performance

Performance is certainly an issue that the editor has absolutely no control over, except for deciding which performance works best in the edited story. You cannot fix bad acting or bad direction of good actors. You can only try to hide it or mask it as much as possible. Sometimes there just is nothing else to cut to and there are no "better" takes to use. Cut in what you think works best for the overall scene, grin and bear it, and move on. If the talent performance is actually very strong but their ability to match their **business** (holding a glass or cigar, brushing their hair, etc.) is what makes a certain take less appealing, be ready to cut in the best performance and let the discontinuity of the little business ride.

Be Familiar with All of the Footage

Reviewing and assessing the footage for quality issues and gauging useability at the very beginning of the editing process actually serve a two-fold purpose. Obviously this will help you "pull the selects" or set aside your best shots for use in the assembly edit. It also forces you to become familiar with all of the footage shot for the project. This is exceedingly important because it will be your job to know what options you have during the cutting process.

For scripted fictional narrative stories, you are guided by the script and footage usually matches that closely. Use the best of what you have to follow the script's framework. As the editor, though, you are often given the ability to rework entire scene order and restructure the story a bit differently than what the script called for originally. You are paid for your storytelling abilities, not just as an assembly monkey. Additionally, if you are working with documentary, news, or even "reality" TV footage, you will have to be rather familiar with everything that is shown (the actions or **B-roll**) and with everything that is said (interviews and so forth). You never know which piece of footage will turn a good edit into a great edit. As you begin to frame the story during the edit, the footage itself helps give it form, direction, influence, etc. An editor familiar with all of his or her building blocks can construct a better project.

So How Does All of This Help You?

The job of the editor goes well beyond just slapping together a few pictures and sounds with a song and a title or two. The editor is the person at the end of the creativity chain who takes all that has been done before (all the production footage, etc.) and puts it together in such a way that it makes sense, tells a story, gives information and/or entertains. An editor is a storyteller who also has to possess technical knowledge, not just of the editing tools he or she uses to conduct the edit, but also of film language — the grammar of the shots.

This chapter has presented you with a review of the simple shot types (i.e., long shot, extreme close-up, etc.), what they look like, and how they may be understood by the viewing audience. These basic shots evolve into complex and developing shots as soon as the production team ups the ante and introduces zooms, pans, dolly moves, and so forth. You have also become familiar with a short list of criteria upon which to base your judgments of "good" or "no good" where the footage is concerned. Knowing what not to use in your edited piece is almost as important as knowing what to put in it. Understanding film language and the ability to scan footage for compromising quality issues are important first steps in becoming a good editor.

End of Chapter Two Review

1. Coverage provides the editor with different views of the same actions for better choices of showing the scene unfold.

2. The basic shot types are extreme close-up, big close-up, close-up, medium close-up, medium shot, medium long shot, long shot, very long shot, extreme long shot, two-shot, and over-the-shoulder shot.

3. Simple shots with only small subject movement become complex shots when there is a zoom or a pan/tilt action. Complex shots become developing shots when you add camera mount movement as well as more elaborate subject movement.

4. Reviewing your footage for best technical and aesthetic qualities will help you pull your selections for the assemble edit.

Chapter Three
When to Cut and Why?

QUESTION: Is there ever a right way or a wrong way to make an edit?

ANSWER: Yes and no.

Editing a motion picture is more than just assembling a bunch of shots one after the other. It involves the creative placement of various picture and sound elements such that when the entire package is viewed by an audience it is able to impart information, entertain, or inspire. This last statement really highlights a fundamental aspect of any motion picture (whether it is a feature film, a TV commercial, a situation comedy, a music video, etc.). The main purpose behind any edited project is for it to be shown to an audience. So as an editor, you are tasked with crafting an experience that will impact a viewer in whatever way the producers of the project intend.

The material for the project was written with an audience in mind, the footage was recorded with an audience in mind, and you must edit it together with an audience in mind. And this is not just any audience, but the specific audience that the project is targeting. A movie about the pranks at a college fraternity may not be seen by the same people who would watch a documentary about late nineteenth-century North American textile mills. Understanding audience expectations and their degree of involvement in the program will be an excellent skill to develop during your editing career. Anticipating the needs of the viewer will go a long way toward aiding your approach to editing the material.

Of course, different genres of motion pictures, different genres of television programming, etc., may all require different editorial approaches. Different content and different target audiences will necessitate different editing styles, techniques, effects, and so forth. While you are starting out on your filmmaking journey and your editing career path, you should be watching any and all of these motion image products so you can begin to see how they are treated, the common approaches, the presence or lack of certain aspects or elements, and so on. Over time, you will most likely develop a solid interest and rather strong skill set in just one of the programming formats (commercials, documentaries, feature films, news, etc.) and you will do the majority of your editing in that genre.

But before we get embroiled in such specifics about the future job you might have, let us return to the goal of our book, which is discussing the basic grammar of the edit. Although it is true that different editing jobs will call for different editing techniques, it is also true that there are some common attributes to most styles of editing. These common attributes are the elements that your viewing audience (including yourself) will look for when watching a motion picture. People are rarely conscious of these elements, but through viewing film and television imagery over time, they subconsciously know how to "read" certain edits and they can easily decipher meaning in the flow of images across the screen. So just as the basic shot types have meaning in the language of film, how an editor strings those shots together in the motion picture also has meaning to the viewer. There is a grammar of the edit.

What Factors Help Make a Transition a Good Edit?

In Chapter One we introduced the four major types of transitions that are used at a cut point in a motion picture: cut, dissolve, wipe, and fade. Each one of these transition types enables the editor to move from one shot to the next. We will discuss what may cause an editor to choose from one of these four transition types in the next chapter, but for now, let us explore something even more basic. What factors or elements compel an editor to want to make an edit in the first place? Why cut from one shot to another very particular shot at that very moment in time?

The following list is meant to serve as a jumping off point. These criteria are some of the major reasons for considering a cut when dealing with most material, but, as with many moments in the filmmaking process, other factors not mentioned here may come into play. Using this list will put you in very good shape when editing decisions need to be made.

- Information
- Motivation
- Shot composition
- Camera angle
- Continuity
- Sound

Information

A new shot should always present some new information to the viewer. In a motion picture, this may primarily be visual information (a new character entering a scene, a different location shown, an event whose meaning is not quite known yet, etc.), but it may also be aural (**voice-over narration**, the clatter of horse hooves, a speech, etc.). A smart editor will ask himself several questions: What *would* the audience like to see next? What *should* the audience see next? What *can't* the audience see next? What do *I wish* for the audience to see next?

Remember, one of the many tasks set up for the editor is to engage the audience both emotionally (to make them laugh, cry, scream in fright, etc.) and mentally (to make them think, guess, anticipate, etc.). Asking the previous questions can generate clever or less-than-straightforward ways of showing the same story. In a mystery you may purposefully show misleading information and in a romantic melodrama you may show the audience information that the characters do not yet know. Regardless of the kind of information presented, the fact that it is there to engage the audience, get them involved, and get them thinking helps keep them interested in the motion picture. When an audience member is thinking and feeling they are not paying attention to the physical act of the edit and this engagement helps keep the movie running strong and smooth. It also means that the editor has done his or her job well.

It must be understood then that this element of new information is basic to all editing choices. Whenever one cuts from one shot to another, one has to ask that if there is no new information in the shot that is being cut to, then why is it being cut to. Is there a better choice? Is there another shot perhaps, from the same scene, which does provide new information and fits into the story as required? No matter how beautiful, cool, or expensive a shot may be, if it does not add new information to the progression of the story, then it may not belong in the final edit.

FIGURE 3.1   Each shot presented to the audience should be providing them with new information about the story to keep them engaged and attentive.

Motivation

The new shot you cut to should provide new information, but what about the shot that you are cutting away from? What is the reason to leave that shot? When is a good time to leave that shot? There should always be a motivation for making a transition away from a shot. This motivation can be either visual or aural.

In picture terms, the motivating element is often some kind of movement by a subject or an object in the current shot. It could be as grand as a car jumping over a river, or as simple as a small movement of a face. Perhaps a character in close-up only moves his eyes slightly to the left as if looking at something off-screen. Editing logic would hold that you could then cut away from his close-up and cut to the object of his interest. The motivation to cut away comes from the movement of the actor's eyes. The reason for cutting to the next specific shot, let us say of a cat, is to provide the audience with new information. It shows them what the man is looking at.

If you wish to use sound as a motivating element, then you would need to address the editing of both picture and sound tracks more precisely near that transition. In its most simplistic usage, the sound could be generated by something visible in the shot currently on the screen. As an example, a man standing in a kitchen in a medium long shot (MLS) watches a tea kettle on the stove. The kettle begins to whistle. The sound of the whistle starting in the MLS can motivate a cut to a close-up of the tea kettle showing steam shooting up from the spout causing the louder whistle (see Figure 3.2). It should be noted that because the close-up shot actually magnifies the visual size and importance of the tea kettle, it can be appropriate to raise the volume on the sound of the whistle in your audio track as well. This lets the size of the visual object influence the volume level of the sound that object is producing.

Changing this scenario slightly, let us now say that the man is sitting at his dining room table in a medium shot. The tea kettle begins to whistle but the tea kettle is not visible within this medium shot's frame. You may then cut to the same close-up of the tea kettle that we used in the previous example, again with a louder whistle on the new shot's audio track. In this case, the audience will accept the domestic whistle sound of the tea kettle even though they do not see the tea kettle. The pay off, and new information, comes when you cut to the close-up of the tea kettle proper. The audience does not notice the transition from one shot to the next because they are processing the information and it makes sense in their knowable universe.

A third and more advanced way of using audio as a transition motivator is rather conceptual in its design. An editor may create what is called a **sound bridge**. A sound, seemingly generated by something not seen or known to the audience, begins under shot one. It motivates the transition into shot two, where the origin of the strange sound is **revealed**. To modify our tea kettle example slightly, let us say that we are seeing the man in the kitchen with the tea kettle in the MLS. The audience begins to hear what they may interpret as the tea kettle whistling. This motivates the cut to a shot of an old steam engine train's whistle blowing. The sound of the train whistle acted as a motivator to leave shot one and it acted as a bridge transitioning the viewer into the new information and new location of shot two. The audience does not notice the unexpected transition because the new visuals of the train whistling give them information to process and it follows a knowable logic (see Figure 3.4E and F).

Motivation

FIGURE 3.2 (A–B) Motivation for the cut comes from the movement of the man's eyes. (C–D) Motivation for the cut comes from the audio track of the tea kettle whistling. (E–F) Motivation of the cut to new information, new location comes from the sound bridge of the train whistle beginning under shot one and carrying the viewer along into shot two.

Shot Composition

Although the editor cannot control the composition of visual elements in the shots that he or she is given to edit, the editor can certainly choose what two shots get cut together at a transition. Provided the correct composition is in the visual material, the editor can help make the viewing of these images more engaging for the audience member. In its easiest form, an editor's choice can be to simply edit in all the footage from one beautifully composed and recorded shot — simple, complex or developing. The beautiful, well-balanced shot was designed to be a show piece, it looks great and plays well once cut into the program. The audience is given the time to appreciate the shot for what it is as it unfolds in its entirety, and their experience is enhanced. Everybody is happy.

Another simple technique is to take two basic but properly composed shots and transition them one after the other. A two-person dialogue presents the perfect scenario to demonstrate this. Your scene starts with a wide shot of two people having a discussion sitting across the table from one another. As character A speaks you cut to a medium close-up of character A. He is sitting frame left with his look room open across frame right. Now as audiences have grown to expect, you will wish to cut away to character B listening. You do cut to a matching medium close-up of character B. She is sitting over on frame right with her open look room across frame left.

Even though you in no way created the individual medium close-up (MCU) shot compositions, you use the alternate placement of characters frame left and frame right to generate interest in the audience members and cause them to stay engaged with the progression of the motion picture. As you cut from MCU to MCU, the audience is getting to experience eye-line match or eye trace.

When a viewer is watching character A speak over on frame left, their attention is over on frame left. They are aware, however, that character A's attention is actually across the screen over on frame right. When the cut to character B comes, the audience traces character A's eye-line across the empty screen and rests upon the new face of character B over on frame right. The compositional placement of character B should be in such a place as to match the eye-line from character A, so the audience is rewarded for following the eye trace across the screen and across the edit.

Like a tennis ball bouncing back and forth across the court, the eyes of the viewing audience will travel back and forth across the screen seeking the new information from each character as you cut from one shot composition to the other. You want to engage the audience's eye trace without making them search too hard for the next bit of information. Subtle searches will keep the viewing experience interesting, but more elaborate searches may only serve to make it more confusing. Beautiful and multi-layered shot compositions can look great on screen, but be aware of how you cut into and out of them and think of how the audience will locate the new, important information within the more complex visual environment.

FIGURE 3.3 Even traditional compositions like these engage the viewers by asking them to trace the matching eye-line across the empty look room on screen.

Camera Angle

In Chapter Two, we discussed how to review your footage and watch out for shots that may have been taken from two positions on set less than 30 degrees around the 180 degree arc of the action line. This is one of the key elements of a shot that will help you determine if it could or should be cut next to another shot. There has to be reasonable difference in the camera angle on action for two shots to be "comfortably" edited together.

When the shooting coverage is planned for a scene, certain camera placements or camera angles are considered to be the most advantageous, and they are the shots eventually undertaken by the camera crew. Due to factors of time and money, only certain shot types from certain angles will be recorded and the production team tries to fit the most information into the fewest, but best looking frames that they can. But an editor will never know from where around the 180 degree arc the camera was placed to record the actions of the scene until he or she reviews the footage. The editor can only do his or her best to place shots of differing horizontal angles (greater than 30 degrees apart) next to one another in the edit.

The reason for this is simple. If two shots are recorded with similar framing from two, very near angles on action, then their resulting images will look too similar to one another, even though they are slightly different. This similarity will register with the viewer as he or she watches the program and it may appear to the eye like there is a glitch or a **jump** in the image at the cut point.

FIGURE 3.4 Editing together two shots of similar camera angles will cause a jump at the cut point. Differing camera angles and framing will help prevent the "jump cut" in the mind of the viewer.

The expression, **jump cut**, is used frequently in the analysis of editing for motion pictures. In this case, as in most, it simply refers to the fact that while watching the motion images, the viewer perceives a jump, a glitch, or extremely brief interruption or alteration to the pictures shown. In our current example of two shots with angles on action that are too close, we will find that the images of shot one and shot two are too similar in their appearance. The audience will not see them as providing sufficiently different views on the same information. The image in their eyes will merely jump, which they will consciously notice and as a result it will serve to pull them out of the viewing experience, which is something that the editor should almost always try to prevent.

Camera Angle

Continuity

Providing smooth, seamless **continuity** across transitions is a very important element to keeping your edits unnoticed by the viewer. Once again, editors are not responsible for the quality of the footage that they are given, but they are responsible for massaging that material into the best motion picture possible. If the production team and talent did not provide the correct visual performances to transition with smooth continuity, it will be the editor's job to make up for that deficiency in some way in the editing. And to make matters more interesting, there are actually several different forms of continuity that need to be addressed at various points throughout the editing process. Let us take a look.

Continuity of Content

Actions performed by the on-camera talent must match from one shot to the next. Because actors are obliged to make the same actions from one take to the next, and from one camera set-up framing to another, for each shot covered in the scene, one hopes that they did the same thing over and over and over. This is not necessarily always the way it is. The continuity of content must be watched for but may not be easily fixed.

As an example, if the family dog is sitting in a chair during the wide shot of a dinner table scene, then the dog should also be seen in the tighter shots used to show the remainder of the scene. If the dog had been taken off set and there were no other shots with the dog sitting at the table with the family, then, as the editor, you get to make a choice. Do you begin the family dinner scene without the wide establishing shot that shows the dog? Perhaps you start the scene on a close-up of the character speaking the first line. Perhaps you start with a close-up of a plate of food, then move out to a two- or three-shot. Additionally, you have the option of showing the dog in the wide shot and then laying in the sound effect of the dog walking away on the hardwood or linoleum flooring while you show the tighter shots of the family without the dog at the table. Perhaps you cut in a shot of the dog lying on the floor in a different part of the house. Regardless of your approach, you are searching for a solution to a continuity problem.

If a man picks up a telephone in an MLS using his right hand, then the telephone device should still be in his right hand when you next transition into an MCU of him speaking on the phone. If, for whatever reason, the production team did not provide any shots of the man with the phone in his right hand, but only in his left, then you would have to **cut away** to some other shot after the MLS and before the phone-in-left-hand MCU. This will give the audience enough of a break from continuous action so that they can believe the man had time to transfer the telephone from his right hand to his left while he was off screen.

In this case, the cut-away is any brief shot that will provide the appropriate distraction and time filler to allow the audience to make the leap in logic of object continuity adjustment (see Figure 3.5).

So either the footage already contains the proper material to edit with the correct continuity of content, or the editor must create some means of hiding, masking, or "explaining" the visual incongruity. No matter the approach taken, the audience must remain ignorant of the issue or else you run the risk of breaking their belief in the filmed illusion. In this respect, editors are rather like magicians or illusionists purposefully distracting the eyes of the audience to cover the trick of the edit.

FIGURE 3.5   Using a cut-away shot may provide the requisite break from action so that the audience does not consciously notice the discontinuity of the telephone in the man's hand.

Continuity

Continuity of Movement

Screen direction is the movement of talent or objects toward frame right or frame left. This must be maintained as you transition from one shot to the next, if the next shot still covers the same movement of talent or objects. The production team should have respected the scene's screen direction and the 180 degree rule during the shooting of coverage. If they did not, and the shot that you would like to use next that continues your talent's movement contradicts the already established screen direction, then you will have to **insert** a logical shot that will continue the narrative and still provide a visual break from the discontinuity of movement. This other shot, of whatever material you have that fits the narrative flow, will offer the audience a break to allow the character time to reverse his direction in the third shot continuing the previous action.

FIGURE 3.6 (A–B) Talent movement should maintain screen direction across the edit point. (C–E) If you wish to cut together two shots that reverse screen direction, then it may be advisable to use an insert shot to break the audience's attention on the direction of movement.

Continuity of Position

Since the film space has direction as noted above, it also must have a sense of place. Talent subjects or physical objects within the frame occupy a certain space within the film world as well. It is important for the editor to string together shots where that subject or object placement is maintained continuously. If an actor is shown frame right in shot one, then he must be somewhere on frame right in any subsequent shots during that scene. Of course, if the actor physically moves, during the shot, to a different location within the film space then it is logical to show him on a new side of the frame. Cutting together two shots that cause the subject or object to jump from one side of the screen to the other will distract the viewer and the illusion of smooth editing will be broken.

FIGURE 3.7   The physical position of objects within the film space and the shot composition should stay consistent across edit points. This woman appears to jump from screen left to screen right after the cut to the other character.

Continuity

Continuity of Sound

The continuity of sound and its perspective is of critical importance. If the action of the scene is happening in the same place and at the same time, then the sound will continue from one shot to the next. If there is an airplane in the sky in the first shot, and it can be seen and heard by the viewer, then the sound of that airplane should carry over across the transition into the next shot from that scene. Even if the airplane is not seen in the next shot of this sequence, the sound of it would still be audible to the characters; therefore it should still be represented to the viewing audience as well.

Sound levels for voices and objects should be consistent throughout an edited scene. Changes in object distances from camera, within the film space, should also be accounted for through raising or lowering volume levels in the audio mix for those shots. Perspective increase or drop off should be represented.

Additionally, all spaces have a background noise level. It may be soft, deep, high, or loud depending on the environment depicted on screen. This ever present layer of sound is commonly called **ambience**, but it may also be referred to as **atmosphere** or **natural sound** (**nats** for short). It is responsible for creating a bed of consistent audio tone over which the dialogue and other more prominent sound effects and so forth are placed. This extra, uninterrupted sound bed is either lifted from the production audio recordings (sometimes called **room tone**), or it is generated by an editor or **sound design** person from other sources. This ambience track helps smooth out audio transitions when you cut from one shot within a scene to another.

Sound

Because there are too many potential topics, we will consider sound as our last major "good edit" factor or element. Entire books are written on the subject of sound editing in movies and television and awards are presented to people who do it well. We will simply scratch the surface of the topic to provide you with a basis for ideas and plenty of food for thought.

Earlier we discussed the tea kettle scenario as a motivator for the edit. Beyond being a source for motivation, the sound track can also be a great way to comment on something within the film or to juxtapose messages within the film; for example, a woman is seen sitting in a noisy business office in a long shot. There is a cut to her in an MCU. One would expect the noisy business office ambience to continue to be heard under the new MCU of the woman. If the audience is not presented that continuity of audio, they could be pulled out of the viewing experience wondering what happened to the sounds. The cut would draw attention to itself in a negative way.

What if the same scenario occurs except this time there is no office noise after the cut? The only thing to be heard is dreamy, ethereal music that seems to match the calm look on the woman's face. This peaceful music is her internal sound track. The audience is given new information about the internal mental or emotional state of this woman. Somehow, within all of the office craziness, she is staying calm and collected. The editor used sound to draw positive attention to the transition through providing the audience, and the woman, with a break from the office noises (see Figure 3.8).

Alternately, sound can make a statement that goes against the visuals being presented to the viewer; for example, you have an interior shot of a man who tells his friend that he is "going to hunt for a job." The roar of a lion is heard on the sound track and the transition takes the picture to a wide shot of a crowded, bustling city street during commuter rush hour. Animal noises are mixed in the sound track with the busy street ambience. The character from the previous shot, the job hunter, is now out in the wild on the hunt for a new job. An audience would not normally accept the animal sounds played while watching a busy city street, but because it follows the context of the job hunt, the inappropriate animal sounds actually become story-enhancing sounds (see Figure 3.8).

As with our train whistle example earlier, the lion's roar scenario presents another sound bridge. The roar takes us from one shot into another. In these examples, the sound of the next shot is heard before the picture of the next shot. We call this sound leading picture. The opposite holds true as well. You may have the sound of shot one carry under the newly visible picture of shot two. We call this picture leading sound. Perhaps you have a wide shot of a man dropping a bowling ball on his foot. As he yelps in surprise, you cut to an extreme long shot of the tops of trees in the forest. As the sound of his yelp continues under the new picture of tree tops, flocks of birds fly up and away in a sudden fright as if the man's yelp carried so far it scared the birds into flight (see Figure 3.8).

This editing practice of having either picture or sound start early or end late is known as creating a **split edit**, an **L-cut**, or **lapping**. If you think of picture and sound as two separate tracks or footage elements (as they are with both film and video editing), then it is easy to see how you might cut both picture and sound track(s) at the same moment in time. This is called a **butt-cut** or **straight cut** where picture and sound end and begin at the same point in time. Assemble edits and maybe the rough cuts will most likely be all butt-cuts. As soon as you start to finesse timing of shots in the fine cut and you offset the cut point for picture or sound for creative purposes, you are making split edits. One track leads or follows the other. When done correctly, these can make your transitions very engaging for the audience. When done incorrectly, they can put the brakes on pretty quickly (see Figure 3.8).

FIGURE 3.8 (A–B) The sound drops away at the cut to show the woman's inner peace. (C–D) The lion's roar bridges shot one to shot 2, which continues the animal sound treatment. (E–F) The yelp of the man bridges across the edit and laps under the split picture track. (G–H) An example of the butt-cut becoming a split-edit.

Is There a Right or Wrong Reason for a Cut?

Yes and no. As with anything that involves a craft, there are the technical methods and reasons for doing things certain ways, but then there are the aesthetic or creative reasons for doing other things in other ways. How you make an edit and why you make an edit are two different things, but they are always interrelated. You can edit a project as you see fit, but in the end, it will be the viewing audience that decides if your choices were right or wrong. Did the edits work or not? Did the audience notice them or not? As long as you have reasons why you made each edit, you are on the right path. Keeping the various elements mentioned in this chapter in mind and pre-thinking what your audience would appreciate will take you a long way into the world of well-received editing.

End of Chapter Three Review

1. Know your audience and remember that you are really editing for them and their viewing experience.

2. Each shot you transition into should provide the viewer with new information that progresses the "story" of the project.

3. Each transition you create should be motivated by some visual or aural element within the shot you are leaving.

4. Use differing or interesting shot compositions to lead the viewer's eye around the frame so they stay engaged when transitioning from one shot to the next.

5. Present differing camera angles to the viewer within a given scene or sequence so they will not experience the jump cut problem.

6. Ensure, as best as possible, that your transitions conform to the appropriate continuity of content, movement, position, and sound.

7. Sound, whether matching the visuals or contrary to them, is a great tool to enhance or undercut meaning in the story and to engage your audience on a different sensory level.

Chapter Four
Transitions and Edit Categories

QUESTION: What makes for an ideal edit?

ANSWER: An edit that serves the story and keeps the audience engaged.

Now that you know what types of shots you will be given to edit, and what factors need to be considered when you wish to make a solid edit from one shot to the next, we should really shed some light on the most common types of transitions that you will use at those edit points you have determined. As mentioned earlier, we will be discussing the cut, the dissolve, the wipe, and the fade. Each one of these four transitions carries with it its own meaning when viewed within a program. Audiences understand these transitions and have certain expectations around their proper, or should we say, more common usage. We will break down each one and analyze how they play into the six elements of information, motivation, composition, camera angle, continuity, and sound.

The Cut

The cut is the most frequently used transition out of all the transitions considered here. It can be defined as an instantaneous change from one shot to another. When it is made at the correct moment, following as many of the positive edit elements as possible, it is not consciously noticed by the viewing audience. It is transparent. As a result, it is the one transition that the audience has grown to accept as a form of visual reality.

The term cut stems from the very beginnings of motion picture film. The actual strip of flexible plastic that contained the images in individual frames was physically cut, either with scissors or with a straight razor device. So the people who cut film strips were called cutters before they were called editors. Even though computer software is used by most people today to do film and video editing and not scissors, the expression still holds. An editor can be called a cutter and the act of editing a film can still be called cutting. Joining two shorter strips of film together, with either tape or glue, was the easiest, fastest, and cheapest way to make a transition. Hence it was used a great deal. Over the one hundred years since the origins of cinema, the cut has made its meaning pretty clear to all of us.

The cut is most often used where:

- The action is continuous
- There needs to be a change of "impact"
- There is a change of information or locale

It is possible to make good cuts and not so good cuts. If you consider all six of the following elements when you are making the cut, you are much more likely to help yourself make a good edit.

1. Information — The shot that is currently playing, shot one, has provided the audience with all the visual and aural information that it could provide. The editor then cuts to shot two to provide the ever-hungry audience with new information. Ideally, every shot in a program should offer some new information such as a large, establishing view of a location, a close-up detail of a computer screen, the sound of rain falling or a baby crying, etc.

2. Motivation — There should always be a reason to make the cut. Something within shot one leads to the need to display shot two. It could be just a need to show new information. It could be a large action within the frame. It could be as small as an actor's slight eye movement. Perhaps there is a noise heard from within the film space but off-screen.

As an editor progresses at his or her skill, the motivated cut point choices may become easier to make. Time passing will even become a motivator for the cut. These amounts of time are generally not marked down in seconds or frames but take on more of a "gut feeling" unit of time known as a **beat**. The motivation for the cut's timing could be based on this unknowable yet knowable beat or a feeling that it is now time to cut to something different.

3. Composition — When you know how the current shot, shot one, will end you know what the composition of those frames will look like on the screen to the viewer. A good edit will also have shot two display an interesting yet different composition from shot one. If the two shots at the instantaneous cut are too similar in their composition, even though they are of totally different subject matter, it can appear as a visual "jump cut" to the audience.

   Using differences in composition at cut points forces the viewer to immediately engage their eyes and brain and search for the new information in the new shot. As long as they are not too confused by an overly busy composition in the new shot, the viewer does not even notice the actual cut as they get engrossed in experiencing the visual elements of this second shot.

4. Camera angle — Each successive shot cut to should be on a different camera angle from the last. A medium long shot of two people talking in profile should be immediately followed by a single shot or an over-the-shoulder shot from somewhere else along the 180 degree arc. **Punching-in** to a tight medium two shot from a similar angle on the talent would not be a good choice. This is sometimes called a **cut-in** or an **axial edit**. Focal length changes (wide, medium, close shots) may also be considered in new shot choices for this scene, but a cut would require an angle change to be most effective.

5. Continuity — The continuous movement or action should be both evident and similarly matching in the two shots to be cut together. Since the cut is instantaneous, the fluid movement must be maintained across the cut. Human viewers are extremely attuned to discontinuities in action across cuts and they are easily detected and disliked.

6. Sound — There should ideally be some form of sound continuity or sound development across the cut point. If a cut happens within footage from the same scene and location, then the ambience should carry over across the cut. Audio levels should match the visuals' perspective on the screen. If you cut from one location or time to another, then immediate differences in sound type and volume are encouraged to keep the audience on their toes. These are sometimes called **smash cuts**.

The Cut

In the perfect world, each cut would contain strong aspects of each of the above elements, but that scenario may not always be achievable. Your goal should be to watch for these elements in all of your footage, train your eyes and ears to pick up on them and use them as appropriate during your edit process. The cut should be where you always start your **assemble edit** (what some people call the **slop edit** due to how quickly you should be able to just slop the selected takes together), and it is still the fastest way to work. When finely tuned, each cut in your fine cut sequence should be unnoticed by anyone who watches the show. Straight cuts are widely accepted when they work and wildly distracting (jump cuts) when they do not. Develop your editing skill set around solid cuts and you will never go wrong. Play too much with the grammar of the cut and you may run into too many problems with your work.

FIGURE 4.1 (A–B) A cut can unite two shots that represent continuous action. (C–D) A cut may end a sequence and lead the viewer into a new location.

The Cut

The Dissolve

This is the second most common transition in our quartet, and unlike the straight cut, it attracts attention to itself on purpose. As you may recall from Chapter One, the dissolve is defined as a gradual change from the ending pictures of one shot into the beginning pictures of the next shot. This is traditionally achieved via a superimposition of both shots with a simultaneous downward and upward ramping of opacity over a particular period of time. As the end of the first shot "dissolves" away, the beginning of the next shot emerges onto the screen at the same time. You get to see the images overlapping. A dissolve may also be referred to as a "lap dissolve," a "lap," and sometimes a video "mix."

The dissolve is correctly used where:

- There is a change in time
- There is a change in locale
- Time needs to be slowed down or sped up
- There is an emotional appeal regarding the subject in the story
- There is a strong visual relationship between the outgoing and the incoming images

A good dissolve is achieved when as many of the following elements are addressed at the point of transition:

1. Information — Much like a straight cut, the new shot should contain new information for the viewer to digest. Whether the dissolve is condensing time over a long, continuous event, changing time periods or locations, or joining disparate concepts through matching imagery, the second shot into which you are dissolving should offer something new to both the viewer and to the narrative of the program.
2. Motivation — As with all transitions, there should be a precise motivating action or narrative need to apply a dissolve.
3. Composition — The two shots dissolved together should each have compositions at the midpoint that overlap easily and avoid a visual contradiction. You may dissolve opposing compositional frames (shot one = main subject frame left/ shot two = main subject frame right) to unify the images in one, momentary yet well-balanced dissolve framing. You may also dissolve matching frames (called a **match dissolve**) where the composition of the two shots is very similar but they

have different subject matter. An example may be dissolving from an extreme close-up of a character's eye to a close-up of the full moon. The two round objects match in composition and shape as the dissolve appears to the audience.

4. Camera angle — Unless you are collapsing time for one long, continuous event recorded from the same angle throughout, you should really try to dissolve between two shots that present differing camera angles on the action. There are many reasons, however, that will negate the usage of this element when dissolves are concerned. Such an example might be a scene where we get to see one character wander about his apartment waiting for a phone call. It is all shot from only one camera angle. The scene encompasses time from late afternoon to mid-evening with lighting changes throughout. To compress time, the editor dissolves portions of footage all from the same unmoving camera angle, but the audience gets to see the character move about the space over elapsed time.

5. Sound — It is customary to also mix together the audio tracks of the two shots being dissolved in what is often called a **cross fade**. As the picture for shot one is dissolving away gradually under the incoming image of shot two, the audio track for shot one is also fading down (growing quieter) while the audio for shot two is fading up (growing louder).

6. Time — An important element in the efficacy of the dissolve is its duration, or how long it lingers on screen. One second is usually the default duration for dissolves in computer video editing software packages, but a dissolve can last for as long as there is visual material on each shot involved in the transition. In general, of course, the dissolve should last as long as required for its purpose in the motion picture. A quick dissolve of just a few overlapping frames, although not instantaneous like a straight cut, does go by the eye very quickly and can imitate a jump cut if various elements of the edit are not met. A long dissolve can be on-screen for several seconds and may, along the midpoint of the longer duration, appear more like a **superimposition** of the two shots rather than a dissolve.

So the dissolve chiefly allows the editor to play with time. If you were editing a story that involved a **flashback**, you could transition from the last shot of the present time frame to the first shot of the events from the past with a dissolve. Often the dissolve is used to create a **montage** of imagery that condenses events over time; for example, a day at the amusement park is shown through ten shots that dissolve from one to the next, the whole sequence lasting only one minute of screen time. Usually such special treatments of visual material are planned by the filmmakers from the outset of the

The Dissolve

project, but editors should feel free to experiment with dissolving time if they find certain scenes to be too long.

It is important to note that dissolves can also slow down time when accompanied by **slow motion** images. A romantic or maybe an emotionally sad or moving sequence can use dissolves rather effectively to slow down events and give the audience time to view and digest the meaning of the material. It is often said that dissolves are the "tear jerker" transition. As they allow the viewer time to think and feel, they are associated with more languid, somber, or "thoughtful" emotional responses.

Dissolves chiefly have their place in fictional narrative motion pictures, television shows, music videos, etc., but you will be hard pressed to find dissolves in the daily news broadcast on your news channel. As they are understood to represent the manipulation of time, there is little appropriate usage of dissolves in factual news reporting, but even this rule of visual grammar is changing as we move deeper into the media overload of the twenty-first century.

FIGURE 4.2 Frames that represent a dissolve from one shot to another.

The Wipe

The wipe may be thought of as a cross between a cut and a dissolve. It has a duration like a dissolve but it tends to be performed very quickly. You get to see both images on the screen at once like a dissolve but there is usually no superimposition involved. Wipes are meant to be noticed by the audience and often appear in colorful shapes, or with other graphic elements associated with them. Wipes can zigzag, spiral, and move diagonally, horizontally, or vertically across the screen replacing the previous shot with a new shot.

The wipe is correctly used where:

- There is a change in time
- There is a change in locale
- There is NO strong visual relationship between the outgoing and the incoming images
- Projects call for more visually graphic treatments at transitions

A good wipe, often a highly stylized transition effect, does not always have to follow the standard elements that lead to good edits:

1. Information — Certainly the shot wiping on the screen will provide the viewing audience with new information.
2. Motivation — The simple need for an editor to leave one location or one segment of a program can be enough motivation for the use of a wipe effect. Sometimes, if you have no purposeful way of getting from one place or time or one topic to another, you can use a creative wipe to "entertain" the viewer across the duration of the transition and lead them to a totally new time, place, or topic. The long part of the grammar of editing transitions, the wipe is the fanciful way of moving around time and space.
3. Composition — Since the style or shape of the wiping element is usually an interesting graphical composition, the framing of the shots just ending and just beginning around the wipe do not require any special visual connection. With careful planning, however, a clever filmmaker may have conceived of strong vertical or horizontal movements within the shot composition and the clever editor will turn these visual elements into what is called a **natural wipe**. Objects within the action of the **outgoing** picture frames appear to push or pull or in some way "wipe" across the screen, which allows for a cut or a wipe to the next **incoming** shot.
4. Camera angle — Much like the freedom found in the types of compositions around the wipe, there is no real need to adhere to the differing camera angle

rules either. The wipe serves to literally wipe the slate clean from the previous shot and introduce a new deal — camera angles are beside the point, but still feel free to creatively explore your options.

5. Sound — Depending on the type or style of wipe you choose to use, sound can be treated as a straight cut or a dissolve across the transition. Sound may lead the wiping shot or follow after it. One has a great deal of freedom in playing with how the audio behaves during the wipe. Depending on the type of program edited, it is even often appropriate to give the wipe action its own sound effect such as a "swoosh."

6. Time — Just as dissolves happen across time, wipes need to have durations associated with them. Fast wipes can transition quickly from one shot to the next when the tempo of the edited piece necessitates moving the story along. If the edited show calls for slower, more lingering wipes, then they could last for several seconds although this may get tedious for a viewer. Fast and fun is generally the way to go.

The wipe often acts as a filler, or a way to bridge two disparate and otherwise not easily joined segments of a program. In classical Hollywood cinema of the 1930s they were a fanciful, more graphically pleasing way to transition from one place or time to another. They take the place of the more mundane dissolves. They have more pep. In today's visual marketplace, wipes can take on any shape or form and are appropriate to use in all genres.

The Wipe

FIGURE 4.3   The wipe literally wipes one image off the screen and replaces it with a new one. They may be used as fast and fun transitions from any shot to any other shot.

The Fade

Motion pictures or sequences from television programs traditionally begin and end with a fade. If you have ever written or read a script, you most likely saw that the first line is **fade in** and the last line is **fade out**. This means that as a fade in (sometimes called a **fade up**), the screen starts out entirely black and then gradually the black fades away to reveal a fully visible image underneath it signaling that the story has begun. As a fade out (sometimes called a **fade down**), the images at the end of your show gradually fade into a fully opaque black screen signaling that the story has ended. Fades can take on any color, but most often you will see black and very occasionally white.

The fade in is used:

- At the beginning of a program
- At the beginning of a chapter, scene, sequence, or act
- Where there is a change in time
- Where there is a change in locale

The fade out is used:

- At the end of a program
- At the end of a chapter, scene, sequence, or act
- Where there is a change in time
- Where there is a change in locale

For a fade to be most effective, it should address the following elements:

1. Motivation — The fact that the piece is beginning will necessitate a fade in and when you have reached the end of a segment or act, it is acceptable to fade out. That is motivation enough for the fade.

2. Composition — It can be very helpful in achieving a clean fade in or fade out to use a shot that will either begin or end (or both) with a low **contrast** image. Compositionally speaking you would not wish to have large areas of dark and light within the frame area, because as the opacity gradually fills in the image or takes it away toward black, the discrepancy between the light and dark areas of the frame will create an imbalance in brightness and make the fading action appear uneven or poorly timed.

3. Sound — It is traditional to have the sound levels raise up under the brightening picture of the fade in. The audio should also fade down as the picture does the

fade to black or fade out at the end. If a fade out from one scene lingers on the all black screen, it is often acceptable to fade up the new audio of the yet to be seen next segment before the fade in occurs. This is an example of sound leading picture.

4. Time — Like dissolves and wipes, the fade requires an appropriate duration. Depending on the project, they could last anywhere from one-half second to several seconds. Usually you will just feel what the right amount of time is because staring at an all black screen for too long, without any new information on the audio track, will feel off-putting. A good example of when you should listen to your gut and feel the right "beats."

Fades in and out have long been part of film language and a standard tool of the editor when starting or ending any motion picture project. They act as transitions into and out of the dream-like state that is motion picture viewing.

The Fade

FIGURE 4.4 The fade out ends one sequence and leads the viewer to new material as it transitions into a fade in on the first shot of the next sequence.

The Five Major Categories of Edit Types

So far we have explored three categories of shot types, eleven kinds of basic shots, six elements that help make a good edit possible, and four different major transitions. Now we are going to examine five major categories of edit types. None of these lists are exhaustive and these five types of edits are no exception, but in giving them these named categories, we are touching on most of the major kinds of edit that can be performed with most material. There may be no industry standards for the terminology, but the definitions will still apply across the board. Granted, the type of project you are editing will help decide which kinds of edits you will be able to execute. Certain genres call for certain editorial treatments, but most programs could absorb one or more of these edit categories and do well by them.

Our five categories for the different types of edit are

- Action edit
- Screen position edit
- Form edit
- Concept edit
- Combined edit

As mentioned earlier, all edits can benefit from possessing attributes or addressing conditions found in the list of six elements that make edits stronger. Our five categories previously listed are all edits, therefore it would hold that each type of edit should also benefit from the same six elements. Let us examine each one and provide some examples.

The Action Edit

The **action edit** is nearly always a straight cut. As its name implies, this category encompasses edits between shots that depict continuous action or movement of subjects or objects. As a result, this type of edit is also sometimes called a movement edit or a continuity edit. The first shot in the series will show a person performing an action — cut — then the second shot continues that action but with a different framing. Time is unbroken. Movements appear to be smooth and continuous.

As a simple example, in a long shot we could see a man sitting at a library table. He leans forward and picks up a book to read it. In a medium close-up we see the man holding the book so we can read the title on the cover and watch his eyes scan the pages rapidly. (see Figure 4.5)

1. Information — The long shot provides the audience with important information about the location, the subject, potentially the time of day if we see windows or lights on, how the man is dressed, and what his actions are like — slow, quick, normal, abnormal.

2. Motivation — In the long shot, the man will pick up the book in front of him off the library table. The action of lifting the book will be a good place to make the cut. The action is the motivator. Of course, you also have the option of delaying the action edit a bit and using the placement of the book, over the man's face, to motivate a cut in to the medium close-up of the book's title and the man's eyes.

3. Composition — The arrangements of subject, objects, and set dressing within the frame of the long shot create a strong diagonal interior space. There are **foreground**, **middle ground**, and **background** layers. The close-up shot offers a centrally weighted frame with the details of the book taking up most of the space. Although framing the man toward the left may have been more in line with his placement in the wider shot, the title of the book and the appearance of the man's eyes are the most important thing in this new shot, so the centralized framing is working better for the conveyance of narrative information in this case.

4. Camera angle — In the long shot, the camera angle is on a three-quarter profile of the man's right cheek. In the close-up, the camera has moved around the arc and approaches his face from a much more frontal framing. The difference between the camera angles of these two shots is more than adequate for the cut.

5. Continuity — The most important aspect of the action edit is the continuity, and the continuity of movement really should match at this cut point. The coverage in

The Five Major Categories of Edit Types

FIGURE 4.5   The motion of raising the book to read it motivates the cut on this action edit.

the long shot does provide the action of the man raising the book up off the table and opening it in front of his face. The close-up repeats that same overlapping action of the book raise and open, plus it continues along with the man's eye movement across the pages. As the editor of this action edit, you would be free to cut and match the movement of the book at any point during the action. Since you cut on action, the audience is not perceiving the cut, but merely registering the presentation of new information about the book and about the man's eyes.

6. Sound — Because this is a library scene, the ambient sounds will be rather sparse, but there should always be some sounds associated with the background of the location; perhaps a "sniff" or a "clearing of the throat" here and there, plus the "hum" of the light fixtures. You could even address the sound of the book pages turning once you move in to the close-up shot.

The action edit is quite common and can be used in very elaborate action hero chase scenes or in very quiet, slow-moving melodramas. As long as there is a continuous action or movement in the frame, the editor can use that to match the same action from another shot of coverage in the scene. If the cut addresses the six elements listed above, it should be smooth, unobtrusive, and allow an uninterrupted visual flow for the story unfolding on the screen.

The Screen Position Edit

This type of edit is sometimes called a directional edit or a placement edit. "Directional" because the edit helps direct the viewer's eyes around the screen, and "placement" because it is the unique placement of subjects or objects in the two shots cut together that make the viewer's eyes move around the frame. The screen position edit can be either a cut or a dissolve, but it is usually a cut if there is no passage of time implied by the edit.

The way the shots of a scene are originally conceived (through storyboards or script notes), composed, and recorded will help an editor to construct a screen position edit. Two shots in the coverage were designed to lead the audiences' eyes around the screen. Usually one strong visual element occupies one side of the frame and casts its attention or a movement toward the other side of the frame. Cutting to the new shot, the object of attention is usually shown on that opposite side fulfilling the viewer's need to see something occupy that visual space.

Serving as the most basic example of a screen position edit is the traditional two-person dialogue scene. Beginning with a medium long shot, two people, in profile to camera, face one another and have a conversation. The standard coverage would call for solo medium shots and maybe medium close-ups of each of the two characters. When it comes time to edit, you could go from the wider two-shot into the solo medium shot of character A who is shown standing frame left. While speaking he gestures with his hand toward frame right. You cut to a matching solo medium shot of character B who is shown standing frame right (see Figure 4.6).

The new, closer shot of character B yields new information for the audience. The gesture by character A, or even the line of dialogue being uttered would be a fine motivator for the cut. The mirrored **composition** is truly the linkage to the screen position category, since the audience had their eyes over on frame left for character A and then had to move them across the screen at the cut point to observe character B in the new shot. The camera angles around the shooting arc are significantly different. Continuity of dialogue delivery is met by the cut, which also means the sound is continuous as well. Not every screen position edit will address all six of the edit elements, but the more the merrier.

FIGURE 4.6 The screen position edit in its most basic form. One subject stands frame left while the other occupies space over on frame right in the next shot.

The Form Edit

The form edit is best described as a transition from a shot that has a pronounced shape, color, dimension or sound, to another shot that has a matching shape, color, dimension, or sound. These types of edits are usually preconceived during the writing or pre-production phase because the visual elements that will match require the correct treatment of composition and, sometimes, screen direction. Rarely is the form edit just blind luck on the part of the editor.

If using sound as the motivation, the form edit can be a straight cut, but in most cases, the transition will be a dissolve. This is particularly true when there is a change of location and/or perhaps a change in time from one shot to the next. The term **match dissolve** is often used to describe this type of form edit.

A simple scenario will serve to demonstrate a form edit. In a story about a man returning to his small, rural village, a series of close-up shots were taken of a jet plane tire, a car tire, a bicycle tire, and a wagon wheel all spinning counterclockwise as they travel over the ground. The four round shapes are framed roughly the same size with a central placement in the shot composition. Essentially they all match. As the editor, if your goal is to condense the man's travel time, you could dissolve from one tire shot into the next until you ended up with the close-up of the wagon wheel. You could then cut to a shot of the man sitting among some goats and dried corn stalks in the back of a mule drawn wagon (see Figure 4.7).

The audience will understand that the dissolving transitions are condensing time. The technological de-evolution of the wheel shapes will show the audience that the man is moving further into the rural area of his home village. The consistency of shape and composition helps keep the viewer's eye trained on the center of the screen and allows them the focus needed to understand the meaning. The sound elements will also digress from very loud to rather quiet as they cross fade into one another under the corresponding dissolving pictures supporting the audience's sense of location and "climate" change.

Form edits are also often used in advertising and television commercials. In thirty seconds it becomes difficult to say your message, so most often advertisers try to show their message in more easily understood graphical ways. Take, for instance, a commercial for an anti-smoking campaign. The **spot** calls for a studio shot of several cigarette packages standing up on end in a field of endless white. One package is the most prominent standing up in front of all others. During the spot, this shot dissolves into a shot of headstones at a cemetery. Each cigarette package was standing in the exact spot where a grave marker is standing in the second shot (see Figure 4.7).

An audience will most likely draw one conclusion from this form edit — that smoking cigarettes may lead to an early death. Whatever the perceived message of the advertisement, the use of the form edit (match dissolve) is what helps the audience to interpret meaning. The shapes are simple rectangles. The compositions match exactly. The juxtaposition and the imagery "union" during the dissolve generate a rather clear meaning and convey the advertiser's message smoothly and succinctly. Provided the duration of this form edit's dissolve was long enough, and the audio tracks worked together, the audience would flow easily from one shot into the next thanks to the matching forms.

FIGURE 4.7 (A–D) The form edit of the wheels dissolving quickly takes the audience to new locations. (E–G) The form edit of the packages and the headstones generates a meaning in the mind of the viewer.

The Concept Edit

The concept edit may stand alone as a purely mental suggestion. These types of edits are sometimes called dynamic edits or idea edits. The concept edit can take two disparate shots of different content and through the juxtaposition of these visual elements at that particular time in the story, they can generate implied meaning not explicitly told in the story. This type of edit can cover changes in place, time, people, and even in the story itself, and it can do so without any obvious visual break for the viewer.

The Five Major Categories of Edit Types

Most often, the concept edit is planned by the filmmaker from an early stage of picture development. He or she already knows that the two separate shots, when joined together in the narrative at a certain point, will convey a mood, make some dramatic emphasis, or even create an abstract idea in the mind of the viewer. It is rare, but not impossible, for an editor to create a concept edit from footage that was not intended to form a concept edit. Be forewarned though that these types of edits can be tricky, and if the intended meaning is not clear to the viewer then you just may have contributed to an unwanted interruption of the visual information flow.

The previous example of the cigarette packs and the gravestones is very much like a concept edit. The idea that smoking may be bad for you stems from the picture of the cigarettes dissolving into the gravestones. Using one may lead to the other.

Another example of a concept edit would be the following scenario. Two couples are out on a date and one woman announces to the group that she and her boyfriend are now engaged to be married. One man turns to the newly engaged man and asks, "So how does it feel to be getting married?" — CUT TO — close-up of a television screen. An old black and white prison movie is playing and the inmate wears shackles around his ankles — CUT TO — wide shot of engaged man and woman, sitting on a couch watching the movie (see Figure 4.8).

Neither shot has anything to do with the other. The group shot of the couples at the restaurant is, in no way, connected to the close-up shot of the old prison movie. The six elements need not be applied here. It is not the elements in the shots that make the concept edit, but the effect of what happens in the viewer's mind when these two shots are joined together at that time. Clearly the engaged man is having some second thoughts about the concept of marriage.

The Combined Edit

The combined edit can be a difficult edit to come by in edited programming because it requires a good deal of pre-production planning on the part of the filmmaker. It would be rare that two, unplanned shots, could be massaged into a combined edit by the editor alone. The combined edit combines two or more of the four other types of edits. One transition may be an action edit combined with a screen direction edit, and there may be a form edit and concept edit all in one.

FIGURE 4.8 The concept edit conjures an idea in the mind of the viewer through the juxtaposition of seemingly unrelated shots.

Consider a children's fantasy story where young brothers are playacting in their pajamas just before bedtime. They are pretending to fight off some goblins with a flashlight and a pillow. One brother tosses the flashlight to the other — CUT TO — a sword landing in the hand of the second brother, now clad in battle armor, standing on a narrow ledge in a cave fighting off real goblins (see Figure 4.9).

If planned well and shot properly, this scenario has many elements that will make it a good candidate for a combined edit. First, the action of tossing the flashlight across the room makes this an action edit. Second, the screen position of the flashlight and sword is similar. Third, the forms of the two objects are similar — the flashlight and the handle of the sword. And lastly, the concept of the power of imagination may be gleaned from this edit. The boys at play actually transition into the heroes of their fantasy.

FIGURE 4.9 The combined edit takes on multiple attributes of several other edit categories.

The Five Major Categories of Edit Types

Will I Be Quizzed on Any of This?

Most likely not. The job of the editor is not to memorize the six elements of good edits or the five types of edit categories as presented in this book, but to use the reasoning behind these concepts to inform his or her choices while making the edits. Knowing that cuts, dissolves, wipes, and fades are made in different ways, have different meanings, and can convey different experiences to the viewing audience is very important. Joining shots together at the right time, in the right way, for the right reasons is really what your goal should be. Knowing the grammar of the edit will help you to better execute the edit. This, and practice over time will enable your skills to develop even more.

End of Chapter Four Review

1. Straight cuts are great for continuous action, when there needs to be a change in "impact," and when there is a change in plot point or location.
2. Dissolves are used to help change time or location, draw out an emotion, or where there is a strong visual relationship between the outgoing and incoming imagery.
3. The wipe can be used to jump in time, jump in location, unite two totally unrelated shots simply to move the "story" along, or just because the project calls for a more graphically vital presentation.
4. The fade in begins a program, scene, or sequence. The fade out ends a program, scene, or sequence.
5. Action edits join shots that cover continuous, uninterrupted action or movement.
6. Screen position edits, through well-planned shot composition, purposefully draw the audience's attention from one side of the screen to the other at the cut point.
7. The form edit unites two shots with two similarly framed objects that have similar shapes or movements. This is usually executed with a dissolve to show the audience how the objects look alike.
8. The concept edit unites two seemingly unrelated visual shots at a certain point in the story and the result is an idea, concept, or message in the mind of the viewer.
9. The combined edit is still just a cut, dissolve, or wipe at one transition, but it combines elements of several of the edit types. These make for rather powerful storytelling moments.

Chapter Five
General Practices for Editors

QUESTION: Aren't the rules of editing made to be broken?

ANSWER: No, they are made to be followed, and, perhaps eventually, creatively reinterpreted by you.

The material in this chapter will brief you on some of the major guidelines for any edit session. Over time, these practices have evolved a bit but they basically stay true to their original intentions because they hold up so well no matter what the project or what the editing fashion of the day may be. To established editors, these guidelines may seem quaint or simplistic, but we are looking to provide some basic ideas for you, the new editors, so that you may absorb these concepts and also move forward with your careers.

These general practices may be considered the starting point at which you begin to consider your approach to editing any material, but they are not the only points, nor are they the end point. We want you to think on your own as well. The common grammar presented gets everybody on the same page, but your creativity and your skill with your editing craft can overrule the grammar. That said, however, you should always be conscious of the rules that you are attempting to bend with your innovation.

The general practices of editing to always consider are as follows:

- Sound and vision are partners and not rivals
- A new shot should contain new information
- There should be a reason for every edit
- Observe the "action line"
- Select the appropriate form of edit
- The better the edit, the less it is noticed by the viewer
- Editing is creating

Sound and Vision are Partners and not Rivals

This seems somewhat obvious, but it is surprising how many editors allow the sound to "fight" the picture. Sound is a partner in the production and must be edited with the same care and attention to detail as the visual elements. The ear and the eye work in unison, supplementing information to each other, so any conflict between the two will cause confusion.

Aural information should extend and expand the message and story of the visuals. It should give information that enforces and supports the shot. For example, if a shot shows a car passing a road sign "Airport," then by adding the appropriate airport sounds (jet engines, etc.), the visual message is enforced and, consequently, more easily understood by the audience. You deliver a multi-sensory experience and you support, or enhance, the picture. A large truck, for example, demands the sound of a large engine.

In its most simplistic terms, it could be said that an editor should never have a picture on the screen with sounds that do not match. The reason for this is that sound can more quickly create reality than vision. The eye tends to take what it sees factually, whereas sound can stimulate the imagination in a more direct way.

Consequently, stimulating the ear to help the eye is one of the basic tasks of the editor, but if the sound directly contradicts the vision, the result will be confusion and rivalry in the mind of viewer — unless, of course, this is the creative intention of the filmmakers.

An editor should always remember that sound and vision are both tools to be used to help show and tell the story. Picture can get in the way of sound and vice versa, but if one should dominate a shot or scene it should be the result of a conscious choice made by the editor.

A New Shot Should Contain New Information

This general practice is one of the elements of the cut and also one of the elements of the dissolve. It is almost important enough for it to be called a "rule."

The success of a good program is based on the audience's expectation that there will be a continuous supply of visual information. This supply, if it is correctly delivered, will constantly update and increase the visual information the viewer has of the events of the program.

There Should Be a Reason for Every Edit

This convention is linked with *motivation*, one of the six elements of the cut.

If the shot is good and complete in itself, with a beginning, a middle, and an end, then it may not serve much purpose to cut a section out and replace it. Especially if the overall result is not better or more interesting and does not fulfill the expectations of the audience even better than the original shot. In short, do your best not to cut apart a shot that stands on its own, intact. Sometimes the best choice for an editor to make is to not cut a shot at all, but simply time its entrance and exit within the sequence.

This does not mean that a three-minute monologue from one person to another should not be edited visually. If one person is listening, then that person is likely to make some form of facial or body reaction to what is being said. These **reaction shots** should be shown to help break up the continual, verbal assault of the one character and to provide new information about the listening party (see Figure 5.1). If, however, the person is talking to himself, and there are no reasons to add flashbacks or to reference other shots, then this uninterrupted monologue may stand unedited. Cutting up a shot such as this just so the audience should have something else to look at is a poor motivation and may only serve to break the monologue and disturb the audience. If the shot is boring, the fault may lie in the type of shot or the shot composition, the script, or the actor's performance.

In recent history, a very fast paced editing style has become rather widespread. Some call this the MTV effect thanks to the quick cutting of many of the music videos once found on that cable network. This tendency has developed alarmingly to where a shot lasting more than three seconds is viewed by some producers and directors as "boringly long." Quick cuts can be very effective, but they have their place like all styles.

FIGURE 5.1   For long monologues, you may wish to cut in a reaction shot to help keep the viewer interested in the proceedings.

It obviously depends on the type of production, picture content, and viewing habits of the expected audience. What is acceptable in an action sequence is not acceptable in a love scene. The reason to make the edit should be worthwhile and visible to all. If you capitalize on the motivation and the reason for the edit, the edit will then seem more "natural."

Finally, in deciding the length of a shot, it is essential to give the eyes enough time to read and absorb the visual information. If you are questioning the "proper" duration for a shot, then you could describe, in your mind, what you are seeing in the shot. When viewing the example in Figure 5.2 you could say to yourself, "There is a house in the hills, there is smoke coming out of the chimney, a man is walking to the house, it is evening because the sun is setting. Cut!" And that is the length of the shot.

FIGURE 5.2   One method of deciding shot length is to talk out the basic description of the shot content. If your eyes and brain require that much or that little time to digest the image, then most viewers will comprehend the visuals at about the same rate.

There Should Be a Reason for Every Edit

Observe the Action Line

The **action line** (or axis of action) is a mental guide for both directors and editors. It is the imaginary line that cuts through the area of action along talent's sight lines or follows in the direction of an object's movement. With it one establishes the 180 degree arc around the recorded subject. It dictates from which side of that subject one is able to shoot. Editors must make sure that the shots they use in the final edited version stay on the correct side of the line and therefore maintain the established screen direction for the scene.

Crossing the line results in a visually contradicting situation for the audience. They are confronted with a different viewpoint of the action and this will change their perception of what is happening. It will, in essence, flip-flop the orientation of left and right within the film space (see Figure 5.5).

For example, if a car is traveling from right to left across the screen in shot one, then the action line becomes the direction of movement. If another shot is taken from the other side of the line, and that shot is then cut next as shot two, the car will appear to be going from left to right as if it immediately turned around in its screen direction. In the film's reality, of course, the car is actually going the same way all of the time. Cutting these two shots together, one from the first side of the line and one from the other, will break the visual flow and the viewer will be confused and will ask, "Why is the car now going the opposite way?" (see Figure 5.3).

The editor must only select shots from one side of the line unless the line is seen to change, for example, if the car changes direction on screen during one of the shots.

The line also exists for people. A two-shot will establish frame left and frame right, therefore also establishing screen direction, look room, and lines of attention for the two characters. Character A is looking toward frame right and character B is looking toward frame left. Any coverage single shot, such as a medium shot or a medium close-up should keep the characters on the same sides of the screen and looking in their appropriate directions. The two shots would edit together well (see Figure 5.4).

However, if one of the shots, perhaps the single shot of character B, was shot from the opposite side of the established line, then that person would also appear to be looking toward frame right. Clearly, with both persons looking right, they would appear to be talking to some third, but unseen, person off-screen. It just would not make sense to the audience who would only be able to account for the two characters. Both shots must come from the initial side, along the 180 degree arc, but never one from each side.

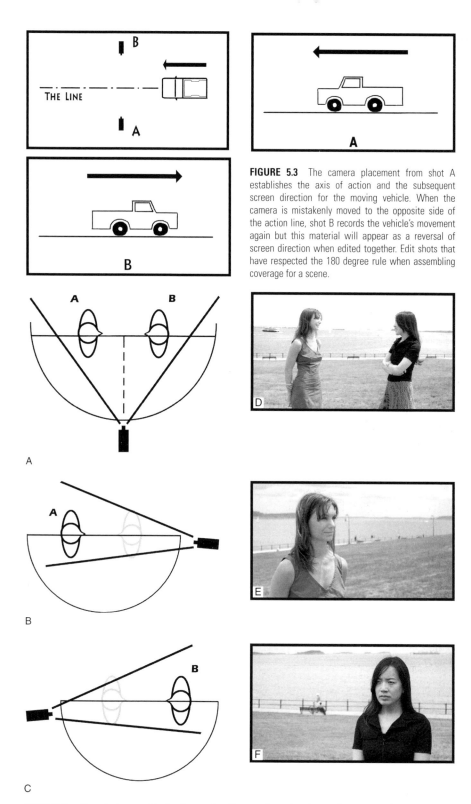

FIGURE 5.3 The camera placement from shot A establishes the axis of action and the subsequent screen direction for the moving vehicle. When the camera is mistakenly moved to the opposite side of the action line, shot B records the vehicle's movement again but this material will appear as a reversal of screen direction when edited together. Edit shots that have respected the 180 degree rule when assembling coverage for a scene.

FIGURE 5.4 Shots that respect the line for people will cut well together. Screen direction is maintained for character A and character B.

Select the Appropriate Form of Edit

If a cut does not create a successful transition between two shots, then it is unlikely that a dissolve or a fade will make it successful. An illegitimate cut is no better than an illegitimate dissolve. Depending on the program edited, it might be possible to use a wipe to make an edit work at an otherwise "sticky" cut point. If a wipe is not appropriate for the show then you are back to square one. Of course, different genres of visual media call for different treatments at transitions. Carefully observe how things are done, replicate them yourself, and then try to break new ground through experimentation. You will find, at times, that certain edits will just not work.

If two shots will not go together as a cut, then they will certainly not go together as a dissolve. This is because either:

- The angle is wrong
- The continuity is wrong
- There is no new information
- There is no motivation
- The shot composition is wrong
- There is a combination of the above

There is very little an editor can do to improve this.

For example, the line has been wrongly crossed as in Figure 5.5. Obviously character B is on the wrong side of the picture. As a cut from one shot to the other there will be an obvious jump. It will jar the audience visually. The "technical" interruption of the images will also then cause a narrative interruption for the viewer and it will not flow smoothly as intended or needed. Clearly, the edit as a cut would be incorrect.

If the editor were to treat this transition between these shots as a dissolve, the edit would be as equally confusing for the viewer. First because the faces of the man and the woman would superimpose over one another during the dissolve, which would make a viewer wonder if this visual treatment were somehow symbolic of the couples union or perhaps there is some supernatural activity at play, and so forth. Secondly, it would be extremely rare for an editor to use a dissolve during any traditionally edited back-and-forth dialogue scene — there is no reason for it. It just does not make sense unless you are emulating classical, shot-in-the-studio soap opera camera switching.

If an edit should be a cut and it fails as a cut, then the failure might be compounded, even more, as a dissolve (see Figure 5.6).

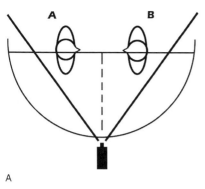

A

D

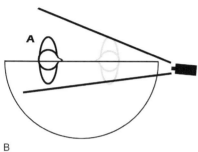

B

E

WRONG SIDE OF LINE

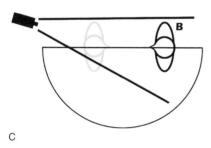

C

F

FIGURE 5.5 Shots that do not respect the line for people will not cut well together. Screen direction established for character A is reversed for character B.

A

B

C

FIGURE 5.6 The incorrect framing of coverage shots will not work as a straight cut and it is made more complicated by the addition of a dissolve.

The Better the Edit, the Less It Is Noticed

This is the ideal situation. A program that is well-edited will result in the edits going unnoticed by the viewer. If the edits are not seen, the story flows from beginning to end.

Sometimes the edits can be very powerful, merely because of the selection of the edited shots. But they will still not be "seen" and as such will help the visual flow. This is the work of a creative editor.

It is equally true that one bad edit can ruin an entire sequence of shots. The general public (not including filmmakers and those familiar with the technical side of motion picture creation) is not likely to stand up, point at the screen and shout, "Hey! That was a lousy edit." What is more likely to happen is much more subtle and also much more insidious. The average viewer, when experiencing a bad edit, will acknowledge the "glitch"; perhaps not consciously, but that visual or auditory blip will register on their brains as something "not-quite-right." As they watch the program after the bad edit, their brain may still be trying to justify what it had earlier experienced at the bad cut, therefore causing issues with the viewer's ability to absorb the new information presented after the bad edit.

Remember, it is your job, as the editor, to create a program that will be pleasing to an audience. If what you do is not to their liking, or presents picture and sound elements beyond the accepted film grammar, they have the right to reject it. If your editing style fits the content of the "story" then they are much more likely to be accepting. As many people are very familiar with this "invisible" technique of film editing (cutting that does not purposefully draw attention to itself), you will not go wrong by working in this fashion. Some of the best edits are the ones that no one notices but you, the proud editor.

Editing Is Creating

As stated earlier in the book, the editor is one of the last people in the creative chain of a motion picture production. It is his or her job to craft the final version of the program from all the rough picture and sound materials provided by the production team. Furthermore, it is the editor's responsibility to make sure that the types of edits fall within the accepted grammar of the program's genre. If the editing style falls outside the traditional audience's understanding, then the program may not be well-received and they simply may not get it.

The general and working practices presented in this book, offer, to the new editor, the rules and guidelines for basic program editing. Everyone should start out understanding why these guidelines exist and then move forward into the realms of play, experimentation, and innovation with the editing styles. There are very well-known, experienced directors who, with their editors, have produced very creditable results in breaking the fundamentals of editing. Some directors have even used the jump cut to a creative end. But this has always been for a special sequence. Breaking the practices to achieve a special result is valid under nearly all circumstances. Certainly, when an editor is seeking to achieve these special circumstances, some general working practices may be changed, ignored, or subverted.

It is usually best to learn these general guidelines and working practices of the following chapter — the "grammar" — before trying to break conventions. But perfect editing grammar is not an end in itself. And if for that reason alone, the greatest working practice of all applies: effective creativity overrules grammar.

End of Chapter Five Review

1. Use sound creatively to underscore and enhance the visual data or subvert it in some clever way and you will provide the audience with a multi-sensory experience.

2. Keep the viewer interested by providing new visual or aural information in each new shot you edit.

3. Find the motivation for each edit. There should be a reason to leave a shot at a certain time and a reason to transition into the beginning of the new shot at its special time.

4. Observe the action line by editing material that holds true to the established screen direction, lines of attention, and lines of motion.

5. Select the appropriate form of edit. Learn when a cut or dissolve or wipe is best and know that sometimes none of them will work to your liking.

6. Good editing often goes unnoticed — this is a compliment so be proud.

7. Learn and understand the basic rules and guidelines of editing grammar and film language, but be prepared to creatively innovate when you know how and why.

Chapter Six
Working Practices

QUESTION: Do you have to memorize all of these working practices?

ANSWER: No, but you should at least be familiar with them. When one of these situations arises on the job you will have a better idea about how to handle it.

Working practices are commonly accepted guidelines, or good tips, for you to think about during the daily process of editing. Some offer specific rules to follow, while others simply suggest some good habits you may consider as you work. You may not encounter these precise scenarios on every job, but you should be aware that they may come up. You will learn how to recognize them and you will find ways to deal with them appropriately. They have been developed over time and they have been found to work within many editing styles and within different genres, but each edit should be viewed with fresh eyes and you will be left to judge whether or not these working practices apply to the project that you are editing.

As many of them are directly derived from the vast grammar of film language, you would be well-served to not stray too far from these working practices unless you find very good reasons to do so.

It should be noted that in today's highly visual media marketplace, there is a multiplicity of motion image offerings. The variety of television programming, webisodes for the Internet, commercials, short films, feature films, documentaries, broadcast news packages, and so forth all require some degree of editing before they are consumed by the viewing public. As you advance in your editing career you will grow to know what each of these program types require for their individual editorial workflow and established styles, etc. Starting with the following section of working practices as a solid base, you will be in a good position to fine-tune and augment your own list of editing "dos" and "don'ts."

Finally, there will be cases where an editor has done everything right — the correct type of edit, the correct elements — so that in theory the cut or dissolve or wipe should work. But it does not. One of the skills of an editor is to analyze and find out why the imperfect edit exists. In such a case, it is possible that the answer may not be found in working practices, but in your own experience or within your own efforts of trial and error. Of course, it could also be that an answer may not even exist. Editing is not a perfect craft. There is always room for creativity and discovery, and that is the beauty of the process.

Explanations for some of editing's working practices are presented here in no particular order of importance.

1. Avoid cutting from incorrectly framed head room to a shot with correct head room (or the other way around).

Reasons

Let us assume that these single character shots are part of an established two-person (or more) dialogue scene. To cut from a shot with correctly framed head room to another shot with incorrectly framed head room will look as if one of the subjects has suddenly altered his or her height.

To cut from a shot with incorrectly framed head room to a correct one and back again will look as if the first subject is bobbing up and down.

Solutions

The incorrectly framed head room shot is nearly impossible to correct. Certain video editing software packages have the ability to resize and reframe the footage, but in this case, enlarging video frames can cause image quality to degrade. Perhaps some of the footage might be usable for cut-aways, if it is not too badly framed. If there is not more than one take of this action or dialogue delivery, the entire shot might have to be rejected and replaced by another, even if the speaker is not seen to be speaking. An over-the-shoulder two-shot (OTS–2S) may be a solution.

Exceptions

The exception here is when the two shots cut together both suffer from the same bad head room framing. Obviously, if the head room is completely wrong, the shots will not look traditional, but since the editor may not be able to do much about it, throw caution to the wind and go for the shots with the best performance regardless of head room. If the performance is engaging enough, most viewers may not even notice the differences in framing.

2. Avoid shots where spurious objects appear to be too close to the subject's head.

Reasons

This is a question of shot composition that has failed at the shooting stage. As an editor, you will not be able to change this questionably composed image. The

FIGURE 6.1 Beware of head room issues when cutting shots of dialogue coverage.

Working Practices

presence of unwanted lines, shapes, objects, signs, etc., in the shot's background can be rather confusing or distracting to the viewer. It may also result in a humorous reaction not wanted by the filmmakers at that time. If offered such a shot, it is best not to use it if at all possible.

Solutions

There really is no solution to this problem. Of course, if such a composition was done intentionally then it would be appropriate for use.

Exceptions

You may be able to use this shot if it has a very shallow depth of field and the background (containing the offending object) is almost completely out of focus. The only other possible use is in a fast montage, where the shot is seen only for a very small period of time.

FIGURE 6.2   Poor shot composition is not the fault of the editor, but the use of these shots in the final edit does fall under her or his domain.

3. Avoid shots where the side edges of the frame cut off people's faces or bodies.

Reasons

This type of framing may be considered aesthetically unpleasing by many who would watch, but that would not be your fault for you did not shoot the footage. Attempting to use closer shots (medium shots, medium close-up) that have such framing will cause complications for the edit. When the partial face of a character is in one shot and then that same face needs to be cut to for the next shot, it will cause a jump cut or certainly a continuity problem with action, line delivery, performance, or screen direction.

Solutions

Sometimes the shot can be used, but it depends what comes before and what comes after. It also depends on the duration of the shot.

4. Cut matched shots rather than unmatched shots.

Reasons

Shots recorded with a similar focal length at a similar distance from the subject and under similar lighting conditions have a similar depth of field, provided the shots have a similar shot composition and content. As you edit together a traditional

FIGURE 6.3 Partial face compositions like these can make a smooth edit tricky. Try to avoid using footage that contains visible portions of faces unless they are part of a pan or dolly move.

dialogue scene between two characters, you will most likely move in from the wide two-shot to tighter singles or over-the-shoulder shots. This allows the audience to get more familiar with the players and their actions/reactions during the scene.

Established film grammar would suggest that the production team shot matching coverage of each character for this scene (this is not always the case, but let us assume that we have that much accomplished within the footage you are editing). It is possible that you may have been given a variety of shot types for each character (medium shot, medium close-up, close-up, over-the-shoulder and two-shot, etc.). Since matching shots often yield similar frame composition, focus depths, and so forth, an audience likes to see two similar shots cut together as opposed to two mismatched shots within the same scene. It creates a coherency and a flow to the visual imagery when cutting back and forth.

In overhead 1 of Figure 6.4, two people are standing in a landscape having a conversation. Camera positions from placement 1 and placement 2 are at a similar distance from each subject — character A and character B. Both the shots are taken, for example, at a narrow lens angle (telephoto or long focal length) and both the shots are framing a medium close-up. When this is the case, the editor will have subjects roughly the same size in the frame and backgrounds that are both out of focus to the same extent. The audience gets to place its attention on the speaking characters alone.

Working Practices

In overhead 2, the camera position for placement 2 has changed. The shot composition should remain the same — a medium close-up-therefore, at the new camera set-up 2, the lens angle will now have to be wider (shorter focal length). In this case the background may be in focus. Consequently, the editor would be cutting from a medium close-up with an "out of focus" background to a medium close-up with an "in focus" background.

Additionally, the perspective on each character plus the included field of view of background elements will not match.

Solutions

If a selection of good shots is available, then preference should be given to those with similarity in the quality of the backgrounds.

Exceptions

The exception to the practice is where a wide angle must be used to show a subject movement from foreground to background or the other way around. Generally, with significant available light, the wider the lens angle used, the more the picture background is in focus. In other words, the depth of field is greater (see diagrams A in Figure 6.4).

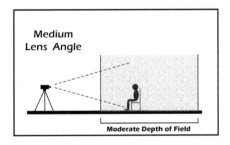

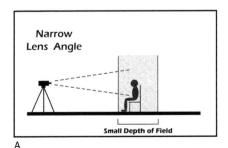
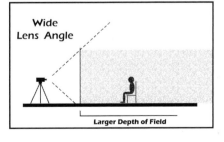

A

FIGURE 6.4   (A) The depth of field changes with focal length.

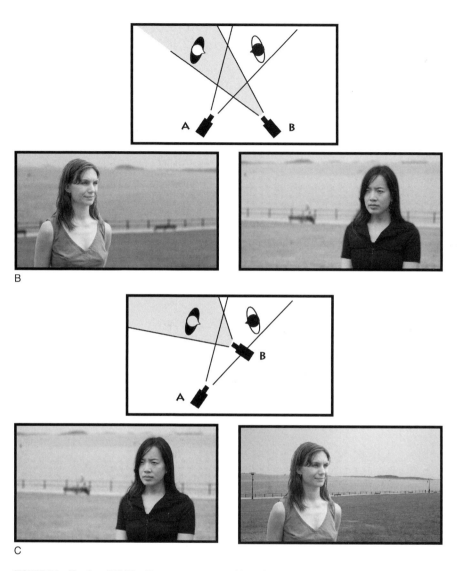

FIGURE 6.4   (Continued) (B) Matching coverage generated by reciprocating camera placement and lens **angle of view**. (C) Mismatching coverage due to altered camera distance and focal length.

5. When editing drama dialogue, never edit out a performer's pauses unless requested to do so.

Reasons

There are some things that can disrupt a performance, and this is one of them. The performer will have rehearsed the script to achieve a certain emotional impact in the scene. Actors rightly claim that the space between words is just as important as the words themselves. To edit out these spaces (or beats or pauses) in a monologue or in a dialogue can change, in the worst case, the complete meaning of the scene.

Solutions

Accept the pauses as a guide and use them as a motivation. Accept the pauses as an important integrated element in the dialogue and not just as a moment when someone is not speaking.

Exceptions

The exceptions are all to do with the lack of time. In news, documentary, short-form commercial, and current affairs programs, where the maximum amount of visual and verbal information must be fitted into the minimum amount of time, the editor may choose to edit out unnecessary pauses.

6. A reaction shot seems more natural during a phrase or sentence than at the end.

Reasons

Remember that each new shot should convey some new information to the viewing audience. During a dialogue scene, just because one person is speaking does not mean that they are always providing new visual information. To help keep the audience engaged, it can be useful to cut to something new such as the reaction shot of the other character listening. Breaking up a long line delivery with the reaction shots of the other character(s) involved in the scene as well as their own line delivery can provide a rhythm to the scene.

If you only show one person speaking, then cut to the other person speaking, then cut back to the first person speaking again, and so on and so on, it will become rather monotonous for the viewer.

Solutions

Look at and listen very carefully to the footage to find a motivation, however small, to insert a cut-away of the listener reacting. If the cut-away is close to the end of the speaker's words, then the cut-away may become the next shot where the second character will actually speak as well. This type of dialogue editing with lapping picture and character line delivery is more interesting to the audience because it shows communication with both actions and reactions.

Exceptions

There are times when a single character does the majority of the speaking in a scene. If the performance is powerful enough to "carry" the scene then by all means leave the line delivery uncut for the stronger emotional impact on the listening audience. Also, there may be a monologue delivered by one solo individual. If that performance is powerful enough, let it ride.

7. Do not be too bound by dialogue when looking for a cut point.

Reasons

In dialogue footage, there are two major possibilities for motivated cut points — vision and words. During a two-person dialogue, action and reaction will take place. If you only cut when one character's words are finished, then it can become predictable or boring. While one person is talking, the other will be listening and may show facial reactions provided that footage was shot by the production team. These reactions are very important and can be used as the motivation for the "back and forth" editing for the scene.

Solutions

In fictional narrative shooting, it is common to record the close shots of one character's dialogue delivery with an off-screen performance of the lines for the unseen character. It will be during these moments that an editor will be able to find the reaction shots for cut-aways. Also, it may be possible to lift some frames out of the beginning of the shot before "action" was called, or from the end after "Cut," if the talent did not break character too early.

In documentary, news, and other "talking head" programming, if no facial reaction is evident during the question and answer period, then the director or producer will hopefully have shot what some people call a reaction noddy of the listener as safety coverage. Noddies are close shots of the listener simulating a reaction to what was said. A noddy may be movements of the head, eyebrows, etc. When noddies are cut into the dialogue with a motivation, they can look quite natural, but they do tip the scales of artifice in news editing.

Noddies are also useful to edit out parts of verbal information. For instance, they can be used to reduce the duration of an interviewee's answer or cover for the numerous "ums" and "ahs" that are inevitably present in the answer and edited out. There is no written rule, but the duration of a noddy should be around four seconds, but could be less depending on the circumstances. Anything too quick (maybe two seconds or less) used as a cut-away shot may seem jarring.

Exceptions

The exception will be when the primary shot is a monologue. There will be no other character present in the scene to use as a cut-away.

8. In a three-person dialogue, never cut from a two-shot to another two-shot.

Reasons

If offered footage of a three-person group dialogue scene which contains two-shots, then in all likelihood the central character will appear to jump from one side of the screen to the other (see Figure 6.5). A shot taken from camera position 1 shows the center person (character B) on the right-hand side of the screen with character A on the left. If you now cut to another two-shot from position 2, then this shot will show the same character B on the left-hand side of the screen, with character C on the right-hand side. This is a screen placement jump cut for character B and can disrupt the visual flow of the shots and confuse the audience.

Solutions

Provided that other coverage shots are available, cut to a single shot of a person instead. For example, cut from a two-shot of characters A and B to a medium

FIGURE 6.5 Three people covered by two two-shots will result in a compositional jump for character B from frame right to frame left at the cut point. Instead, use any other coverage to join to the initial two-shot.

close-up of character C. Or, conversely, you may cut from a medium close-up of character A to a two-shot of characters B and C.

You could also cut back out to a wide shot of the entire trio in between both of the two-shots provided there is appropriate continuity.

Exceptions

There are no exceptions to this practice.

9. On close shots of single characters, the fuller the face the better.

Reasons

As the editor, you do not get to influence what type of coverage shots are recorded during production, but you can choose which shots make it into the final edit. If medium close-up, close-up, or big close-up shots are all recorded for a scene, it is often best to choose the closer shots that show the subject's face more fully depending on the story points of course.

The angle on action will be out of your hands, but if the footage is provided, and depending on the state of the narrative at that moment, you may be well-served by using the shots that show the character's face in either a frontal or three-quarter profile rather than a full profile or a three-quarter back angle. These frontal angles allow the face and its features to be seen more readily by the audience. The face, open toward camera, may then convey more emotion or any sort of reaction. This also keeps the character's eyes visible for the viewer.

The following examples illustrate what may happen if you were given these types of shots.

Example 1 — Figure 6.6

A man is sitting at a desk. A telephone rings, he picks it up and speaks into it. The two pictures are shot from camera angle A and camera angle B. Cutting these two shots together will not produce a jump cut, but the subject's face will be almost totally covered by the telephone. In addition, any words he speaks will not be seen to be spoken, and worse still, any reaction or emotion from the subject will be almost entirely hidden.

Even if the director realizes the error and shoots several takes with the telephone in the talent's right hand (on the opposite side of his head), the information coming from this angle is still compromised due to the full profile. The audience cannot really see into the character's eyes and they cannot really see what sort of facial expressions he might be making while he speaks and listens.

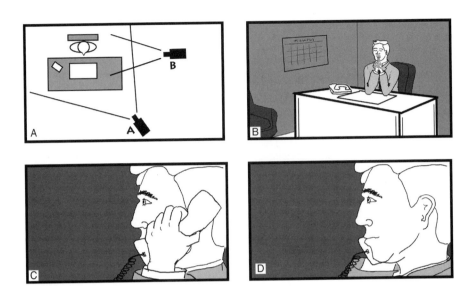

FIGURE 6.6 Whether the phone is on the near or far side of the actor's head, the profile shot deprives the audience of key facial information.

Therefore, this edit deprives the audience of information. Even though it would make a technically good edit, it breaks the flow of the story. You should look for a better angle on the closer shot.

Example 2 — Figure 6.7

In this example both shots are taken from the same position. By choosing the close shot of a fuller face (this is a three-quarter profile), the subject's emotions and reactions can be more clearly recognized.

Cutting these two shots together runs the risk of a jump cut, because the camera angle of the close-up is the same as the camera angle of the longer shot. This is sometimes referred to as a cut-in or an axis punch-in because the camera will be seeing the same subject/objects from the same camera angle and the detail in the tighter shot will simply be a magnification of the same view from the wider shot.

Therefore, editing these two shots together would tell a better visual story (allowing the audience to see facial information), but in technical terms it is less acceptable because of a possible jump cut along the same camera lens axis.

Example 3 — Figure 6.8

If you are provided the footage as seen in Figure 6.8, then you will have little issue making this edit. There is little chance of a jump cut provided there is appropriate continuity of action.

FIGURE 6.7 The three-quarter frontal view of the man's face allows the audience to see his expression while he speaks on the phone. However, keeping the camera in the same place may cause a jump when you cut to the close-up.

FIGURE 6.8 When the production team altered camera angle and focal length, it made your job easier to cut these two appropriate shots together.

The two shots will cut well together for the following reasons: (1) the camera angle of the closer shot is sufficiently different from the long shot, so that the cut will not jump; (2) the subject's face is relatively full to camera, so that all aural and facial reactions will be seen by the audience; and (3) matching the movement of the arm in the wider shot (from A) to the movement of the hand and forearm in the close shot (from B) is much easier than in the other two previous examples. Therefore, this combination tells the visual story better and is technically correct.

10. With a single character, try to avoid cutting to the same camera angle.

Reasons

Much like Example 2 in Working Practice #9, there is a strong chance that a jump cut would result when you edit two shots taken from the same or extremely similar camera angle (see the six elements of the cut in Chapter Three). This relates directly to the film shooting practice known as the 30 degree rule where each coverage shot of the same subject or object in a scene should come from the same side of the axis of action and be at least 30 degrees different in camera placement along the 180 degree shooting arc.

In diagram 1 of Figure 6.9, for example, cutting from the long shot at camera position A into a medium close-up at position B would present problems. Cutting from a medium close-up to the long shot, however, is less of a problem.

Solutions

It would be better to cut to a shot of the medium close-up from a different camera angle, provided one was actually recorded by the production team.

In diagram 2 of Figure 6.9, camera placement B has moved to the right creating an angle on the talent that is more three-quarter frontal. If a shot from this position were available, the cut would be more interesting and the risk of a jump cut reduced.

In the case where an alternate angle shot does not exist, then a cut-away could be used to separate the long shot and the medium close-up of the same character on the same lens axis. This cut-away (of something appropriate to the scene) will allow the audience a visual break and the jump cut effect will not be experienced. This practice is more or less acceptable, if you cut in to the long shot from the medium close-up.

Exceptions

One exception to this practice is when cutting two shots together that are *very* dissimilar such as when a great distance is covered between the two shots set up along the same lens axis. Of course, for creative reasons, one could edit a series of cut-ins along the same lens axis to achieve a quick "punching-in" closer and closer effect.

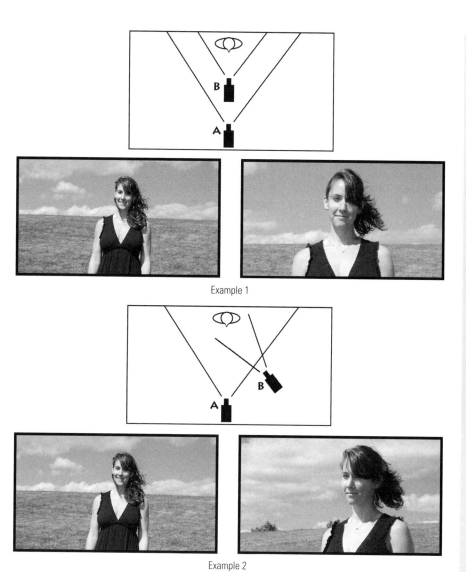

Example 1

Example 2

FIGURE 6.9 Example 1 shows a cut-in or an axial punch-in. Example 2 shows a better shot option for the cut. A new angle and focal length help.

11. When cutting the "rise," try to keep the subject's eyes in frame as long as possible.

Reasons

The rise is any movement of a subject from a lower to a higher position within the frame and across the edit point. For example, the subject sits on a park bench (first shot) and then gets up (second shot). The action edit point may occur anywhere within the actor's total movement.

It would be most advisable to try to keep the actor's eyes on screen for as long as possible in the first shot. The subject's eyes are the natural focal point of the viewer's attention. Therefore, the eyes should be in frame as long as possible. This is especially true in close shots although a rise on a close-up will occur very quickly due to the magnification of the head within the shot's framing.

Solutions

A woman is seated at a park bench. The edit point in shot 1 will be when her eyes approach the top of the screen, frame 1B, cutting to frame 2B in shot 2 (see Figure 6.10). This may seem only a short distance, but actually the subject leans forward before rising. This happens naturally.

If the subject's head is off the screen when the cut is made, frame 1C, then the edit will appear to be "late." If the editor cuts before movement, frame 1A, so that all the movement is seen on the medium long shot, frame 2A, then the edit may be deemed an "early cut."

In these examples, early cuts are not normally as disturbing as late cuts. Watching most of the action from the second (wider) shot is not so wrong, especially if the woman continues up and out of frame. However, the late cut example of shot 1C and shot 2C presents the issue of what the audience gets to look at during the last few moments of shot 1. Granted this transition will occur relatively quickly, but once the entire head clears the top of frame, the audience is seeking some new information. It wants to see the character's face again and watch the continuous action of the move.

Exceptions

One exception to this practice is when the first shot is closer than a medium close-up. It is rather difficult to cut smoothly away from a close-up or big close-up on a rise. An early cut is almost inevitable due to the size of the face within the frame and lack of physical space for the upward movement.

These two shots cut together, but there is no movement, so it is not on the rise.

FIGURE 6.10 Examples of cutting on the rise.

This cut would be better. Notice that the eyes are still in the frame in the first shot.

Now her head has cleared the frame, this would be a late cut.

FIGURE 6.10   (Continued)

12. When editing in a close-up of an action, select a version of the close-up where the action is slower.

Reasons

If the action of the close-up is the same speed as that of the wider shot, then the speed of the action, as seen on the close-up, seems faster. This is due to the relative size of the object within the closer framing. Since it is now a large object it has very little space to move within the close-up framing. Any quick or even "normal" movement would appear to happen too quickly. You are hoping that the production team understood this phenomenon and got some of the close-up takes at a slower speed of object movement.

For example, the subject is picking up a book in the wide shot (see image A of Figure 6.11). The close-up (image B) shows the hand also picking up the book. The action on the long shot is at normal speed and the book never leaves the frame. But in the closer shot the book moves out of frame very quickly. So, if the close-up action is carried out at the same speed, it seems faster.

Working Practices

FIGURE 6.11   Be aware of speed of action in closer shots. Quick movement will not match the wider shots across an action edit. (A) Shot 1 is a long shot of a man picking up the book. (B) Shot 2 is a close-up showing the man with the book in hand.

Solutions

You hope that the director has provided an additional close-up with a slightly slower action. The result of editing in the slower version will appear more natural.

Exceptions

This practice does not apply to shots of moving machinery.

13. Prefer a tracking shot to a zoom.

Reasons

This debate goes back to when the zoom lens (a single lens barrel with multi-focal length capabilities) was first introduced to the motion picture market. Many argue that a zoom has a very unnatural effect due to its magnification of distant objects. It has no change in perspective, so that the horizon (or far distance) and the middle distance will come toward you at the same speed as any objects in the foreground. As our eyes do not zoom, the lens movement will seem unnatural and can break the visual flow.

If you are editing a drama and you are offered a choice between a zoom covering the action and a dolly tracking shot (sometimes called a truck in or a push in), try to avoid using the zoom. A track on the other hand is a natural movement that will have a perspective change and is closer to what our normal vision would produce. Of course, if a filmmaker has it in his or her head that a zoom is the technique they wish to explore for a certain shot, or shots within a scene, then in all likelihood there will be no accompanying dolly shots that achieve similar goals. As the editor, often just a "gun for hire" you will edit in whatever the producers want.

The two sequences of shots in Figure 6.12 show the difference between the zoom and the dolly tracking shot.

It is also a common practice for filmmakers to combine lens and camera support movement within a complex shot. A shot containing a zoom may be used

Zoom   Dolly

FIGURE 6.12 Zoom movements will alter perspectives on the film space, especially the Background. (A–C) Example 1 — zoom movement. (D–F) Example 2 — dolly movement.

provided it contains another camera movement at the same time which helps to camouflage the zoom.

Examples

- Tilt with a zoom
- Pan with a zoom
- Dolly crab with a zoom
- Pedestal or boom elevation with a zoom, etc.

Exceptions

The only other example of the use of a zoom is when it "creeps," i.e., when it is so slow that you actually do not realize it is a zoom. Slow zooms during long takes of slow action or dialogue-driven shots will evolve the composition over a longer time and the subtle changes in framing happen so gradually that a viewer will most likely not notice as they pay attention to the actors, etc. As an editor, this type of shot will be relatively easy to cut in to the program in its entirety, or cut up with other reaction shots as necessary because the zoom will be so slow that cutting on the lens movement will most likely not be noticed.

A zoom in TV news or other "reality" type programming is another exception as they are more accepted within those genres. Obviously a detail of the content is the motivation to make the zoom.

In addition, a zoom in a shot without any discernible background, e.g., a white wall or sky, would be acceptable.

14. Beware of shots that track out without motivation.

Reasons

A dolly **track out** (**truck out**, or pull out) can often signal the end of a sequence or a scene, and therefore may precede either a dissolve or a cut to another scene or even a fade to black. If no character or object movement comes toward the camera initiating the track out (backwards), then the camera takes on a conscience of its own. The audience may not be accustomed to the camera suddenly moving as if it were motivated by its own thoughts or desires and this may cause some disturbance in their viewing associations.

Solutions

The motivation for the track out will usually be included in the shot. In the case where no motivation is evident, or where motivation does not exist in the previous shot, the track out should be treated with extreme caution.

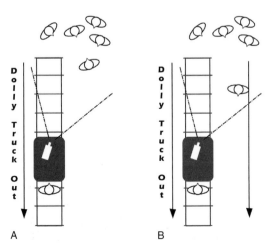

FIGURE 6.13 Use truck out dolly shots that are motivated with character or object movement.

Exceptions

The rare exceptions to this are when a track out precedes a narrative jump in time, location, or tempo, or where the track out is the penultimate shot of the production used partly as a background for superimposed end credits.

15. When editing in a pan or a dolly crab move, use the best version that is smooth, well-timed, and leads the subject's movement.

Reasons

Dolly moves and even panning shots that follow talent movement are often rather difficult to record during production. Several variables and different crew members, plus talent, are involved in their creation and it is easy for things to not quite flow as intended. When reviewing the takes of complex or developing shots like these, watch for the one with smooth camera movement, adequate lead room for the subject's movement, proper focus, and good pacing. An audience member watching a bumpy move, a bad composition, or a blurry moment in the shot will be unimpressed and the viewing experience will be compromised.

Solutions

Again, an editor cannot change the quality of the shots that he or she is given, but the editor must work with the material presented as best as possible. Seek out the best takes that are available that meet the criteria for such a shot. If there are a number of takes, a shot should be selected where the camera has "led the subject" (see Figure 6.14), i.e., where there is more frame space before the subject than behind, has good focus throughout, and is smooth with good pacing (meaning not too fast and not too slow; and if you have to err on one side, choose too fast over too slow; you do not wish to bore the audience).

Exceptions

The exceptions to this practice may be found in fast-paced action shots, or even handheld cinéma vérité style shooting where the slightly "jerky" camera adds to a sense of immediacy, danger, or reality.

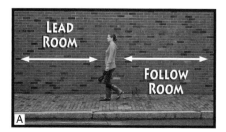

FIGURE 6.14   Select the crab dolly shots that provide ample lead room for talent movement.

16. Begin and end each pan, tilt, or dolly shot on a static frame.

Reasons

Cutting into a shot that is already in motion can cause the jump cut effect within the mind of the viewer. Cutting away from a shot that is in motion to a static shot can also be jarring, but it may be more acceptable if the narrative calls for such an "applying of the brakes" treatment.

Solutions

The production team should provide footage of pan, tilt, and dolly shots that begin with a static frame, move for the duration of action, and then end on a static frame. This is not always the case, but as an editor you would hope for this scenario.

If shot 1 is a static, simple shot and you wish to cut to the complex moving shot (shot 2), then you should keep those static frames at the head of shot 2. This allows you to cut from static frames to static frames. The audience will treat this as an "invisible" edit because they are accustomed to seeing static shots cut to static shots.

At the end of complex shot 2, after the tilt, pan, or dolly move, you will need to finish that shot on the static frames. You may then cut to shot 3, the next static shot. This again provides an invisible edit for the audience — static to static.

Exceptions

If you decide to string several complex movement shots together, perhaps in an action sequence, then you will not be cutting static to static but moving to moving to keep the pace of the action going. One thing to watch out for in this scenario, however, is the speed of the camera movement and the subject movement within the shots you are cutting together. If the speeds are not matching, or at least similar, this can cause visual interruptions to the flow of images and the audience may be turned off.

FIGURE 6.15 Static start frames in dolly shot 2 will help create an invisible cut from the static end frame of shot 1.

17. If the objects or subjects are moving within a pan, dolly crab, or truck, never cut
     to a static shot of the same objects or subjects if they are then stationary.

Reasons

A cut from or into a camera or pedestal movement will appear as a jump to the eye.
An object or subject in movement in shot 1 but who is stationary in shot 2 will
appear as a jump in time or a discontinuous action.

Solutions

Take, for example, a subject within a dolly move (Figure 6.16) who is moving in the
direction of the crab. It is possible to cut to a static shot of the subject, but only when
the subject has cleared the frame for a reasonable time prior to the cut. The dolly of
complex shot 1 should be static prior to the cut to the simple static medium shot.

Special note: There is much debate around how to handle cutting into and out of
moving shots. Generally, the accepted answer is do not do it — at least while
you are still learning the craft.

There are two reasons for this. First is the advice "finish or clear the action in the
shot before cutting out of the shot." Secondly, the perfect pan or dolly is likely
to be a complex shot. As such, like a developing shot, it should have a beginning
(the initial static frame), a middle (the pan with another movement, tilt or zoom),
and an end (the final static frame).

The preferred place for the cut is on the static frame, where the camera is not
moving, even though the subject may be.

So, unless the camera stops, and/or the subject stops, and/or the subject is no
longer in frame, then it is better not to cut to the same subject, if this subject is
stationary.

Exceptions

There are many scenarios where this guideline may be overruled. Depending on the
material involved, the program type, the pacing of the footage, and the scene cut,
you may choose to experiment with cutting into and out of action and stationary
shots. Most likely you will succeed in proving to yourself that it just does not look
or feel right.

18. Objects, like people, moving in a direction have an action line. Do not cross it or
     the direction is reversed.

Reasons

Refer to the section General Practices: Observe the action line in Chapter Five.

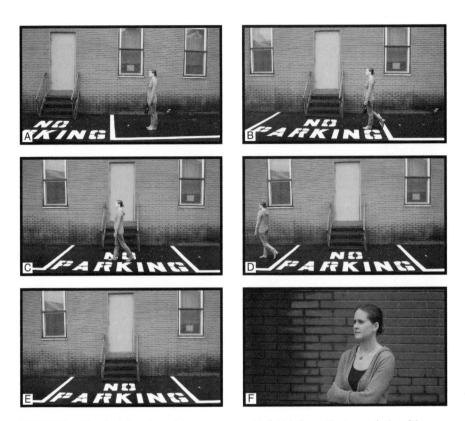

FIGURE 6.16 Allow the dolly action and character movement to finish before cutting to a static shot of the same stationary character.

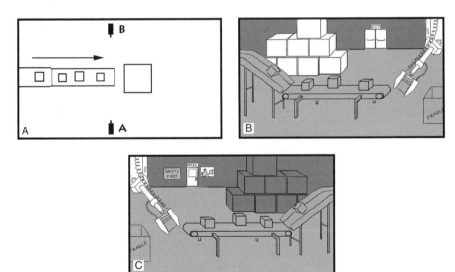

FIGURE 6.17 The machinery establishes a movement and a screen direction. Shooting from the opposite side of the initial 180 degree line would reverse the flow.

In diagram 1 of Figure 6.17, a conveyor belt moves boxes from frame left to frame right as seen from camera position A. The shot itself is shown in image 2.

If the line is crossed, i.e., taken from camera position B (overhead diagram 1), then the belt appears to be moving the boxes from right to left (image 3).

Solutions

Select shots from one side of the line only, or use a suitable cut-away between the shots if the line must be crossed. A close-up of part of the machinery not showing the belt movement would be suitable. In documentary or reality programming you could also use a wipe to get from one side of the belt to the other.

Obviously, if the camera were to move from one side of the belt to the other during the shot, a jump cut will not appear, but the direction of the belt is still reversed.

19. Avoid cutting an action edit from a two-shot to another two-shot of the same people.

Reasons

An action edit requires near perfect continuity. Once two moving actors are involved in the shot, it becomes that much more difficult for the editor to match both characters movement.

Solutions

When cutting out of the two-shot, cut to a closer shot of one of the two characters, cut to some form of reaction shot, or possibly cut to a very long shot if it exists among the footage. Trying to match the action for all concerned parties would be difficult if you went for another two shot from a different angle.

Exceptions

A much wider shot of the entire environment, including the two action figures, is more likely to hide any incongruous body movements and so forth. Any event shot with multiple cameras may also alleviate this issue since action should match across a multi-camera edit.

20. When cutting a telephone conversation together, the head shots should be looking in different directions.

Reasons

Traditionally, film grammar indicates that the characters, speaking over the telephone from two separate locations, will be composed so they look across the empty frame, and from opposite sides. This will generate the idea in the viewer's mind that they are "addressing" one another across the screen as you cut from one single shot to the next and back again.

Working Practices

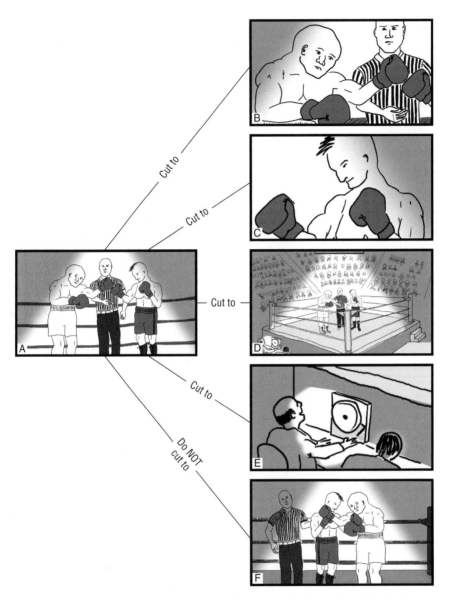

FIGURE 6.18 Cut from the first medium long shot to any other coverage shot but another medium long shot.

Solutions

Hope that the composition of the footage for this scene was done in such a fashion. Otherwise, edit whatever material you have since you cannot alter the subject's placement within the frame.

FIGURE 6.19 Telephone dialogue coverage of two persons in separate locations should be treated as if they occupied the same film space and were speaking to one another in person. Proper framing and look room should be present in the shots.

FIGURE 6.20 Screen direction should be maintained across action edits.

Exceptions

There may be good dramatic reasons to change this working practice. If one person is shot with his or her back directly toward the camera, then the direction of the other person may be changed if the footage allows it.

21. If a character exits frame left, then, for an action edit, the same character should enter the next shot frame right.

Reasons

This is a very basic practice for any moving thing, object, or person within the accepted film grammar. The continuity of screen direction, even across the transition, must be constant. It helps establish the directions of left and right within the film space and keeps the audience properly oriented within this fictional landscape.

Solutions

The appropriate coverage with proper screen direction should be provided to you for the edit. If you do not get the shot with proper screen direction maintained, then you had better seek a diverting cut-away shot to place in between.

Exceptions

The exceptions to this practice are:

- The direction is actually seen to change on screen

- There is a suggested change of direction on screen followed by a cut-away
- The change of direction is caused by the cut-away (i.e., in the haunted house, running in one direction, seeing the ghost, then running the opposite way)

22. Beware of screen placement issues with an "object of interest."

Reasons

Even though the human subjects are on the correct sides of the screen in the coverage shots, the audience will have an additional visual reference, sometimes called the object of interest or the point of interest.

For example, a two-shot of a man and woman (shot 1) shows a painting that is framed center screen. Cutting to the man (shot 2) will show the painting screen left. Cutting now to the woman (shot 3), the object of interest (the painting) has jumped to screen right. Even though the edit is technically correct, the point of interest jumps, and this is visually disturbing.

Solutions

Where an object of interest is evident, either keep it in the same area of frame, or select the shots that either eliminate it altogether by selecting closer shots of one or other of the subjects (shot 4).

Exceptions

An exception to this working practice is where the object of interest is so small as to be negligible, where it is far in the background, or if it is out of focus. Another is where the object of interest is covered, partially or totally, by action.

FIGURE 6.21 Much like a person can "jump" sides of frame in a "back-and-forth" dialogue, objects of interest can do the same thing. Try to keep to closer shots to hide the object jumping.

23. Give a wide shot as soon as possible after a series of close-up shots.

Reasons

It is very easy for an audience to forget the exact location of a scene, especially during a fast-moving production. After a series of medium shots, medium close-ups, and close-up shots, particularly those with "out of focus" backgrounds, it becomes important to re-establish the scene's location. If you choose to introduce a series of characters, all in close-up, then you would do well to show them all again grouped together in the wide shot.

Solutions

Be careful about editing an entire sequence with only close-ups — unless there is a need to do so.

Even one short long shot, showing the relationship of the subjects to each other and to their surroundings, gives a much better grounding to the scene.

Exceptions

The exception to this practice is where the location or scene is well-known to the audience.

24. On the first entrance of a new character or new subject, edit in a close shot of it.

Reasons

The audience will not know the new character or subject, and this may be the first time the character has been seen. The audience needs to absorb a new face and new characteristics. This may be a person, a dog, a robot, and so forth.

FIGURE 6.22 After a series of closer shots it may be helpful to show a wide shot to re-establish the scene in the viewer's mind.

Working Practices

A long shot will only show the character or subject in relationship to other subjects and to the location, but a new character needs to be shown closer to be identified.

Solutions

Edit in a closer shot of the character at the earliest opportunity. This also applies if the character is not new but has not been seen for some time. Support the audience by reminding them of events and people.

Exceptions

The obvious exceptions are when the character is an extra or is a "bit" player or needs to be kept secret for narrative purposes.

25. When editing a new scene with new backgrounds, show an establishing shot at the earliest opportunity.

Reasons

The audience really likes to know not only what is happening in a new scene, but where it is happening.

Some form of geography is required to establish in the minds of the audience the relationship of subjects to the environment that surrounds them.

In short, some form of wide shot, for example, a long shot, a very long shot, or an extreme long shot, will be helpful. This wide shot should serve a number of purposes such as to give some geography of the scene, to show time of day or season of year, to establish the relationship of the character(s) to the surroundings, and/or to establish a general impression of movement of the subjects.

Exceptions

Obviously, if no exterior establishing shot was recorded then you will not have it to edit it in at the beginning of the new scene. You may also opt, for creative

FIGURE 6.23 Appease and inform the audience by showing them a closer shot of a new character entering a scene.

reasons, to not show an establishing shot, but cut right in to the scene, perhaps in a close-up shot of some element within the set. Then you could pull back and show a wider shot of the location of the scene. This method would stress audio ambience over exterior imagery while you are grounding the viewer in the new location, and makes for a refreshing change.

26. Avoid making an action edit from a long shot of a character to a close-up of the same character.

Reasons

It is a jump cut to be avoided, unless a shock effect is required or unless the character is recognizable and identifiable in the long shot.

Example

In example 1 of Figure 6.25, the overhead schematic shows a man walking up to a car in a very long shot. He stops beside the car door to unlock it with his key. In two shots, it may look as it does in Example 1 of Figure 6.25.

It will cut together, but it is too much of a jump to the eyes, and the visual reaction may be, "Who is this new man?," or "Where have the other man and the car gone?" Unless this character and vehicle are extremely well-known to the viewing audience, this edit can break the visual flow and is therefore unacceptable.

It would be better to use three shots as shown in example 2: (1) the long shot to set the scene; (2) the medium long shot at a different angle; and (3) now that he is readily identified, back to the first angle and the close-up shot. The result of having the extra shot in between the two shots is to make the scene flow easier. Now the audience knows where the man is going and what he is doing.

FIGURE 6.24 Using a wider shot to open a new sequence of scenes at a new location can help ground the audience and provide much needed information with one image.

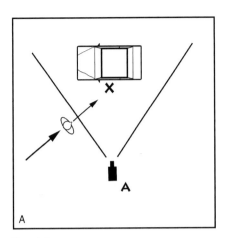

Example 1

Wide shot from Camera A

Close-up shot also from Camera A

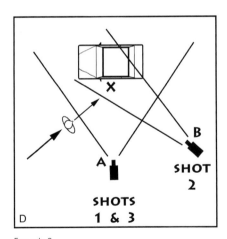

Example 2

Shot 1 — Wide shot from A

Shot 2 — Medium long shot from B

Shot 3 — Close-up from A

FIGURE 6.25 If the coverage has been provided, you may find it necessary to cut in the medium long shot of the character closer to the vehicle so the audience follows along with this series of action edits.

27. Beware of editing a cut to black followed with a cut to full picture.

Reasons

A cut to black is a very serious statement in narrative film production. Since it is an abrupt change over from visible picture to full black it carries with it a very dramatic weight, especially when you cut straight out of that black to a new, full picture. In the days of actual emulsion film editing, a cut to black, followed by a cut to picture, was often understood to mean that a shot was "missing" from the current work print.

Solutions

The possible combinations for the end of a sequence or scene and the start of another are:

- Cut to next picture
- Dissolve to next picture
- Fade to black, fade up to picture
- Cut to black, fade up to picture
- Fade to black, cut to picture

Exceptions

The cut to black and cut to picture is used to break two entire programs, or two productions or two complete items from each other, or for a very dramatic effect.

28. At the start of a program, the sound track can lead the visual track.

Reasons

Some editors claim that a picture without sound is dead, but sound without a picture is not. An audience, upon hearing the sounds (possibly music and ambience), will begin to imagine what is happening even before they know anything about it. The imagination is triggered. As the pictures then come on the screen, the multi-sensory experience begins.

Obviously this practice depends upon what the sound is and what the opening pictures are in the program.

Exceptions

In short form (30 to 60 seconds) television advertisements, where the picture is obviously on screen as early as possible for time reasons.

29. For the end of a program, use the end of the music.

Reasons

Music, of whatever nature, usually is divided up into different passages, verses, or segments and will have a distinct structure. Part of this structure will be an ending or climax. This climax should be used to match the end pictures. It would be confusing to show the final pictures of a program with an opening musical passage. They just would not match.

Solutions

The music should be **back timed** to find its correct start point relative to the visuals of the sequence. If the timing is correct, the last bars of the musical piece should match the final shots of the sequence. This is especially true at the end of a program when the last bar of the music equates with the final caption and the fade to black.

Exceptions

The main exception to this practice is where the music is faded gradually into or under other sound, dialogue, or music that is stronger than the first.

30. Put aside your edited piece for a while and watch it again with fresh eyes.

Reasons

When you are an editor of a feature film or any long-form documentary piece, etc., you become "married" to the movie. You live with it day in and day out, sometimes for months at a time. You are often listening to the same sections over and over and over again. You grow to anticipate the words and the pictures until they no longer really stand out in your mind but are part of the editing "wallpaper." It becomes very easy to blind yourself to edits that are not working or entire sections that may be better in another location within the sequence.

Solutions

Time allowing, you would be wise to take a break from the editing process. A day or two away from the well-known material will help you forget the exact pacing, the cut points, the lines of dialogue, and so forth; perhaps not forget entirely but you will be watching the piece with less anticipation. This respite should give you a pair of "fresh eyes and ears" to view and listen to your story. When you approach the same material with fresh senses, you may pick up on what edits are not working and which scenes within the piece may play better elsewhere.

Exceptions

Obviously, if you are involved with much shorter or more straightforward cutting jobs that have a "quick turnaround time," then you will not have the luxury of taking a day or two away from the material to refresh your senses. You will hope that an overnight break will be enough time away for you to be more critical of your own work come morning.

31. Use close-ups of characters in a scene for greatest impact.

Reasons

The close-up of an actor's face is a very intimate shot. It carries with it a great deal of visual information and, depending on the expression of the face and the context within the story at that point, it can sway an audience. Using such a powerful shot too early in a scene's development will dilute the efficacy of those same shots when they are used later to make an emotional point or underscore a certain counter-current in the storyline.

Solutions

Save the close-up shot of the character or characters for when an audience will benefit most from seeing the actors' faces so large or looming. If the drama or tension of the scene is rising, cutting to closer shots toward the climax will provide the audience with juicier visuals. The close-up will yield an easier assessment of a character's emotional or mental state to the viewer. This effect will be watered down if you go to the close-up shots too soon in a scene's development.

Exceptions

Documentary and news "talking head" interviews will be recorded mostly in medium shots and closer. You will have to use these shots right away in the sequence. Often, fictional narrative television programming will have coverage shots with more close shots of individuals due to the smaller screen on which they get displayed. Cutting to such shots sooner in each scene may even be encouraged for television programming.

32. Cut away from a character as soon as his "look" rests upon his object of interest.

Reasons

A shot depicting a character looking at some object of interest off screen is the perfect set-up for a **reveal** to the audience. In general, one would cut to the shot of the object of interest next. The motivation for this edit rises out of the character's look and initial facial reaction to the yet-to-be-seen object off screen. Once the physical movement of head and eyes has come to a rest the audience will likewise wish to see what is now being focused upon, hence the cut to the object's shot.

Solutions

The editor hopes that the actor was instructed during production to look off screen and react to some object. He or she further hopes that the talent achieves the look with a final solid head placement and **eye-line** to some object off screen. It is the solidity of the final look — the focusing of the eyes along a particular line — and a facial reaction of recognition that create the strongest cut point.

Exceptions

Clearly, if no take of the looking shot ends with a solid, strong gaze from the actor then you cannot cut away at the eye's focus point. You will have to simply try to find the most acceptable point of recognition on the actor's face and then cut. Faster action sequences or scenes that involve multiple objects off-screen would not necessarily call for a static head and focused eye-line from the actor.

33. In documentary programming, edit out "ums" and "ahs" in interviewee speech.

Reasons

Often your goal as an editor, especially in documentary programming of real people, is to make them look and sound as good as possible on screen. A mother of a football player, a diplomat, or a scientist may all have certain verbal pauses in their vocalized speech patterns. They may say "umm" or "ahh" to fill the space between their thoughts. While listening in person, these verbalized pauses often go unnoticed unless they are extremely excessive. Watching a short answer filled with "umm" and "ahh" will be more noticeable and less appealing to the viewer.

FIGURE 6.26 Allowing the actor's eyes to lock on the off-screen object of interest generates a need within the viewer to also see this new object. The cut to the object of interest is often called a reveal.

Solutions

Edit out these verbal pauses whenever possible. If the mouth does not move very much while the sound is made, try to cut in **room tone** for those few frames. If the offense is more visually noticeable, then you may have to cut away to a graphic or some **B-roll**, or to an interviewer "noddy" shot if such a thing exists.

Exceptions

Occasionally, someone's speech pattern and the verbal "ticks" they may exhibit are inextricably tied to their persona. It will be best to keep these inherent pauses to provide the viewer with the full "flavor" of the individual's character.

34. In the audio track levels, make sure music does not overpower dialogue.

Reasons

Music is a very powerful creative device. It can propel a scene forward, slow it down, make the audience feel sad or happy or tense and so forth. Once you get your program to the point where your music bed is in place, it will be important to regulate the sound levels so the music does not compete with the dialogue or other audio tracks in your piece.

Solutions

Attend to the proper audio level mixing for all audio elements, especially the music. If the music is **diegetic** (generated within the film world by a radio, band, CD player, etc.) then be aware that it should play continuously under that scene until the music ends or the scene does. If dialogue is delivered on top of the music bed, then make sure to lower the music level under the spoken words. An audience will accept the fact that the music level drops because they are usually more interested in what the people have to say.

Exceptions

Clearly, if the location sound is recorded for a live event (concert, benefit gala, etc.) then it will be difficult to impossible to lower the captured music levels in the background. Also, if the fictional narrative story calls for the loud music to drown out the spoken word, then keep it hot in the mix for this special purpose.

35. Use cleanly recorded dialogue under off-screen or over-the-shoulder line delivery.

Reasons

During production, the **sound recordist** may not have the **boom operator** favor the off-screen or over-the-shoulder "shoulder" talent, which means that their dialogue will sound weak while the favored talent's line delivery given in the shot will sound strong.

Solutions

Say that the actor whose face is visible on screen is character A and the actor whose face is not visible is character B. For the audience to hear the off-screen or over-the-shoulder non-favored line delivery of character B, use only the audio track from a clean take when character B actually is on screen in his or her own medium shot or close-up. This means finding a shot in the coverage where character B's picture and sound were recorded, but only use the sound track from that shot underneath the other picture of character A's single shot or over-the-shoulder with character B. This will provide clean, clear audio for both characters during the scene no matter what series of shots get edited together.

Exceptions

There really should be no exceptions to this guideline. You should always strive to start with the cleanest, clearest, strongest audio signal when you are editing the sound elements for a program. If the sound needs to be modified (made worse) for a special effect within the story, then you should still start with clean sound and degrade it yourself in a controlled fashion.

36. Be aware of proper durations for inter-title and "lower third" graphics.

Reasons

Just as a recorded shot of a person can stay on screen for too long, so can a title or other graphic element. The audience absorbs visual information from the shots based on composition, lighting, character facial expressions, colors, etc., but they absorb information from **inter-titles** and identifying **lower thirds** by reading it. If a title is not on screen long enough, it cannot be read and understood. If a title is left on screen for too long, the audience may become bored waiting for the next shot or the next bit of information.

Solutions

An inter-title that says, "Later that same day…" (only four words) may be on screen for as little as three seconds. An inter-title that consists of several short sentences may require 10, 20, or more seconds depending on how many words and how complex the visual presentation may be. A general guideline for the editor is to leave a title on the screen for as long as it takes to read through the words three times in a row. This is dependent upon length of written word of course and may have to be averaged down or up depending on the importance of the title and the overall timing of the edited program. Inter-titles, traditionally white lettering over a solid black background, are often preceded by a fade to black and followed by a fade from black.

Lower thirds, usually showing a person's name, occupation, or location in news or documentary programming, should come on at the bottom lower third of the screen just a bit after the closer shot of the person speaking has been cut to. It should stay on screen long enough for the information to be read and digested by the average person and then it should go away. Often lower third identifying titles like this dissolve on to the screen, stay solid, and then dissolve off — a bit less harsh than a straight cut on and off. It is also customary to use the lower third identifying title on the first appearance of a person in a program. There is no need to show the title again if the same person is shown again.

Generally speaking and on average, most titles may live on screen at full opacity anywhere from three to ten seconds. It would be advisable, however, for you to get feedback from several other people who know the project so you can gauge how they feel about the timing of the title elements and lower thirds. Often one-half of a second longer or shorter will make a big difference in making it feel "right."

Exceptions

There are no real exceptions to this general practice. As the editor of these created graphic elements, you have total control over how long you wish to leave them on screen. After you know the information has been conveyed, it becomes a question of "beats" to determine the appropriate duration.

FIGURE 6.27 Titles and lower third graphics require appropriate timing for each edited piece. Too short and the audience may miss out on information — too long and they may get impatient waiting for the next visual bit.

37. If applicable, make a cut at a loud sound on the audio track.

Reasons

Loud sounds are known to cause many people to blink their eyes.

Solutions

If used wisely and with discretion, an editor may be able to find a point in a scene's development where a loud sound will occur on the audio track. If the picture edit is made at this point, it is likely that the cut transition will be hidden during the blinking process of the audience members who are reacting to the loud sound. This is a bit of a cheat and a bit of a gamble, but it may be effective at the right moment and for the good of the overall project.

Exceptions

One should not cut just any time there is a loud sound on the audio tracks. This is a poor way to construct a good story flow.

38. Take advantage of the transition point that natural wipes offer when they occur in the footage.

Reasons

Natural wipes occur any time an object moves past the camera lens and momentarily blocks the composition of the frame before it clears out. The movement provides the perfect motivation to make a cut or a wipe to a new shot in the same scene or to start a new scene.

Solutions

Really thoughtful filmmakers will actually pre-plan the talent blocking of main characters, or more often "extras," to create the natural wipe moment for the editor to use. Other times, a simple happenstance like a van driving through the shot on a long lens exterior set-up can provide the motivation and the physical "blockage" for the editor to create the natural wipe on his or her own initiative. Regardless of who constructs it, the natural wipe is natural because it is occurring within the recorded shot while it happens — inherent to the footage. Sometimes, during a complex dolly shot, the camera may crab past columns or pillars in a hotel lobby or a parking garage structure. Even though the objects are solid and unmoving, the camera's movement past them will create a natural wipe on the recorded images. These are convenient and clever transition points for the editor to use.

Exceptions

Just because the natural wipe occurs, it does not mean that you must avail yourself of it and cut or wipe at that point in the footage, especially if it does not add to the overall scene.

FIGURE 6.28 An editor can take advantage of the natural wipe within the footage and either cut or wipe to a new shot at that time.

39. Take advantage of the transition point that whip pans offer when they occur in the footage.

Reasons

Much like the natural wipe, the **whip pan** (or **flash pan**) offers a very convenient and visually interesting motivation to transition from one shot to another. If planned by the filmmaker ahead of time, the fast motion blur generated at the end of a shot as the camera quickly spins horizontally will match with a corresponding motion blur at the start of another shot which is supposed to follow. The editor will join the tail blur of shot A to the head blur of shot B and the illusion, when watching the transition play itself through, will be that the motion of the blurring whip hurtles the viewer into a new location or a new scene.

Solutions

These whip pan shots (and much less frequently whip tilts) are usually designed and shot on purpose by the filmmaker during production. Unless there is a great deal of handheld footage that whips quickly left or right, then there will be little opportunity for an editor to create their own whip pan moments.

Exceptions

Not all whip pan transitions will play correctly. The tail of shot A and the head of shot B must be whip panning in the same direction and roughly at the same speed for this transition trick to work.

40.   Avoid cutting pans and tilts that reverse direction at the cut point.

Reasons

Screen direction and flow of motion have a continuity of their own. When object movement motivates a leading camera pan or tilt in shot A and then shot B reverses that object's movement, a visual "crash" will occur at the cut point. Screen directions will have suddenly switched and the viewer will feel the push or pull of disorientation of visual flow.

Solutions

You will hope that production maintained screen direction and visual continuity while they were shooting the coverage for the scene. If you do not have a continuous direction in the footage between shot A and shot B then you can either not use shot B or insert some other shot between the two to distract viewers and re-orient their sense of movement so that when shot B comes on the screen, they are not disturbed by the alteration in the pan or tilt's direction of movement.

Exceptions

As a creative practice, it may be worthwhile, given the appropriate topic in a program, to attempt to marry reversing pan or tilt shots to cause the visual crash for effect.

41.   When possible, show your edited program to someone else and get their feedback.

Reasons

A project worked on for many hours, days, or sometimes months, can become stale to you over time. The fresh eyes of other individuals may help you see weaknesses that you could no longer objectively notice.

Solutions

It is advisable but not necessary for an editor to show his or her work to other people to get their feedback. Just because you, as an editor, think something really works does not mean that it will play the same way for others. Often, showing your work to other people will bring up points that need to be addressed, edits that do not quite work, and even places that are rather successful. Listening to and acting upon the critical feedback of other people will be an essential skill that you will need to develop as an editor. You may feel that you have done everything right, but the opinions of others bear a certain weight as well — especially if they are paying your wages.

Exceptions

Unless you live alone in an igloo near the Arctic Circle, you should always make time to have other people review your edited piece. No one should work in a void.

42. Advance the physical motion by a few frames at the head of the second shot in a continuous motion action edit.

Reasons

A viewer understands the concept of continuous motion. Something moves through space across time. Faster movements across shorter spaces occur over faster time. The "blink" that is the actual edit from a wider shot of the coverage of action to the closer shot of the continuation of that same action eats up a tiny amount of time in the viewer's mind. Therefore, a few frames of action/time can be left off the head of the second shot.

Solutions

Perhaps this can be best demonstrated with an example. The simple scene involves a man sitting at a restaurant counter. As he reads his newspaper, he lifts a mug of coffee and drinks. Shot A is a wide shot of the man at the counter — he reads his paper and lifts his mug of coffee — CUT TO — shot B, a medium close-up shot continuing the coffee mug lift and shows the actual sipping of the beverage.

Once you decide where to cut away from the motion path of the man's arm rising in shot A, you will be better informed as to where you will begin shot B. Rather than trying to match exactly to the frame the place along the rise where the arm should be in the medium close-up shot, you should move forward in time by a few frames and have the arm be a bit further along its path at the beginning of shot B. In other words, the mug should be a bit closer to the man's mouth in the second shot of the action edit.

Experiment with cutting action early, cutting exactly the same, and cutting a little later (as in our example) and judge for yourself. Most continuous action will benefit from fewer frames at the head of the second shot. The motion flow feels more natural to a viewer this way.

Working Practices

FIGURE 6.29 Cutting into the second shot a few frames later in action will most often make for a smoother transition across the action edit. Viewers understand that time has elapsed just enough during the cut to the new information.

43. Keep your rough cut long, do not be tempted to do a finely tuned edit early in the process.

Reasons

No matter what kind of programming you are editing, this guideline applies. Keep your material longer in the first pass or two of the full construction of the show. Without knowing overall pacing/timing issues or scene ordering issues, it will be hard to make final decisions about shot, scene, and sequence length. You will be better able to judge what can come out after the entire assembly has been viewed a few times. If it were already missing, you may also have missed out on a better creative opportunity.

Solutions

From the outset, you should include everything from picture and sound tracks that you feel will help properly show/tell the story. At that early stage of editing you really do not know what will be useful or superfluous, so keep it all in. After a pass or two at the entire piece, you will get a much better feel for what works and what does not, what should stay and what should really go.

Often you have much more material than the final **running time** of the program will allow (30-second commercial, 15-minute educational video, 30-minute situation comedy show, 2-hour feature film). Some things that were initially included in your first versions of the edit will stand out as unnecessary. Other times, you will have to make hard choices that call for removing very good pieces just to make the final running time cut-off. Regardless, you should always start with the most material and then pare it down … that is what editing is all about.

Exceptions

Some news packages have extremely short air time and you will not be able to pad out the first cuts and then tweak. You will most likely have very little time to

FIGURE 6.30 A dissolve across these two shots will help make a connection between them in the mind of a viewer. The old farmer is like a sleeping dog.

finesse and you will simply have just enough time to cut something together to get it to air in the right time slot.

44. Use a dissolve between *simile* shots.

Reasons

Two shots that may not have anything in common within the context of the present scene or story can behave like a simile. The dissolve will unite the two different shots and a new meaning is created in the mind of the audience. A straight cut would not unite the subjects of the two different shots; therefore the audience may not understand the filmmakers "literary" intensions.

Solutions

Sometimes a filmmaker wishes to make a visual simile with two distinctly different shots. As you may know, a simile is a comparison of two disparate subjects using the words like or as. In our example, we compare the retired, old farmer to the sleeping old dog. Although the old dog is part of the narrative, a cut to him may not create the sought after visual connection. A dissolve to him and back to the old man would unite them and allow the audience to understand the visual simile.

Exceptions

This sort of visual simile treatment has its origins in the silent cinema and if used today can often feel heavy handed. Through the use of sound and other, less obvious, visual elements, one might be able to convey a similar connection.

45. Use insert shots to cover gaps in continuity or condense/expand time.

Reasons

There will arise a need in every editorial process where continuity of action, direction, or dialogue is not quite right across certain edits. There will also be a need for the editor to condense or expand time to help the pacing of a scene.

Insert shots and **cut-away** shots will help with this. They divert the audience's attention enough from the previous shot without breaking out of the content of the scene in which they appear. The momentary distraction usually serves as enough of a visual break to reset the attention of the audience on the next cut that continues the action or dialogue after the hidden glitch.

Solutions

The editor will hope to have footage specifically shot for cut-away use or he or she will have marked certain shots that contain usable insert moments: close-up of a dog, a clock, a photograph, a reaction shot from another character in the scene, etc. Keeping these insert/cut-away pieces available will help the editor mask over the continuity issues or help lengthen a moment or condense a longer action by providing a related and believable distraction to the minds of the audience.

Exceptions

Certain footage, for example, from long-winded talking head interviews, that has no B-Roll or other related visual material may not offer any opportunity for insert or cut-away shots. If the project does not have the footage and does not call for use of full-frame graphics or titles, then you may be in an editorial quandary.

FIGURE 6.31 The insert shot of the dog allows time to be condensed so the rider can arrive at the cabin that much sooner.

46. Avoid leaving an empty frame whenever a subject or object leaves frame.

Reasons

Empty frames, even with a background showing and in focus, provide no new
information to the viewing audience. When a person is leaving frame at the left
or right edges, it is best to cut away from that shot before they leave the frame
entirely. It is customary to cut away once the actor's eyes have cleared the edge
of frame, since the face and eyes of the actor are what an audience member will
be watching.

Solutions

As seen in Figure 6.32, leaving shot B with the body or object still partially visible
gives the audience something to remain focused on just prior to the cut.
Introducing shot C, the viewer will find an empty frame (with new visual data to
analyze) and then the actor or object will enter the frame with continuous screen
direction and movement. This allows something of interest to the viewer to
remain on the screen at all times.

Exceptions

You really may not want to leave more of the exiting subject's body on screen at the
end of shot B or at the start of shot C, because with too much body visible in both
shots it will appear as a jump cut.

FIGURE 6.32 If you wish to allow some empty film space at a cut point, make the new or in-coming shot start empty. Even the empty frame will provide new visual data to the viewer before the character strides in from the edge of frame.

End of Chapter Six Review

1. Avoid cutting from incorrectly framed head room to a shot with correct head room (or the other way around).
2. Avoid shots where spurious objects appear to be too close to the subject's head.
3. Avoid shots where the side edges of the frame cut off people's faces or bodies.
4. Cut matched shots rather than unmatched shots.
5. When editing drama dialogue, never edit out a performer's pauses unless requested to do so.
6. A reaction shot seems more natural during a phrase or sentence than at the end.
7. Do not be too bound by dialogue when looking for a cut point.
8. In a three-person dialogue, never cut from a two-shot to another two-shot.
9. With close shots of single characters, the fuller the face the better.
10. With a single character, try to avoid cutting to the same camera angle.
11. When cutting the "rise," try to keep the subject's eyes in frame as long as possible.
12. When editing in a close-up of an action, select a version of the close-up where the action is slower.
13. Prefer a tracking shot to a zoom.
14. Beware of shots that track out without motivation.
15. When editing in a pan or a dolly crab move, use the best version which is smooth, well-timed, and leads the subject's movement.
16. Begin and end each pan, tilt, or dolly shot on a static frame.
17. If the objects or subjects are moving within a pan, dolly crab, or truck, never cut to a static shot of the same objects or subjects if they are then stationary.
18. Objects, like people, moving in a direction have an action line. Do not cross it or the direction is reversed.
19. Avoid cutting an action edit from a two-shot to another two-shot of the same people.
20. When cutting a telephone conversation together, the head shots should be looking in different directions.

21. If a character exits frame left, then, for an action edit, the same character should enter the next shot frame right.

22. Beware of screen placement issues with an "object of interest."

23. Give a wide shot as soon as possible after a series of close-up shots.

24. On the first entrance of a new character or new subject, edit in a close shot of it.

25. When editing a new scene with new backgrounds, show an establishing shot at the earliest opportunity.

26. Avoid making an action edit from a long shot of a character to a close-up of the same character.

27. Beware of editing a cut to black followed with a cut to full picture.

28. At the start of a program, the sound track can lead the visual track.

29. For the end of a program, use the end of the music.

30. Put aside your edited piece for a while and watch it again with fresh eyes.

31. Use close-ups of characters in a scene for greatest impact.

32. Cut away from a character as soon as his "look" rests upon his object of interest.

33. In documentary programming, edit out "ums" and "ahs" in interviewee speech.

34. In the audio track levels, make sure music does not overpower dialogue.

35. Use cleanly recorded dialogue under off-screen or over-the-shoulder line delivery.

36. Be aware of proper durations for inter-title and "lower third" graphics.

37. If applicable, make a cut at a loud sound on the audio track.

38. Take advantage of the transition point that natural wipes offer when they occur in the footage.

39. Take advantage of the transition point that whip pans offer when they occur in the footage.

40. Avoid cutting pans and tilts that reverse direction at the cut point.

41. When possible, show your edited program to someone else and get their feedback.

42. Advance the physical motion by a few frames at the head of the second shot in a continuous motion action edit.

End of Chapter Six Review

43. Keep your rough cut long, do not be tempted to do a finely tuned edit early in the process.

44. Use a dissolve between *simile* shots.

45. Use insert shots to cover gaps in continuity or condense/expand time.

46. Avoid leaving an empty frame whenever a subject or object leaves frame.

Chapter Seven
The Final Cut: Additional Editing Topics You Are Bound to Encounter

---

QUESTION: What is expected of an editor?

ANSWER: These days, much is expected of an editor. Depending on the job size, budget, and purpose, many editors are tasked with performing more than just straight cuts — graphics creation, motion effects work, music selection, and audio mixing may all be part of the modern editor's responsibilities.

Having covered many topics regarding shot type, shot quality, transition types, edit categories, and working practices, we are all in a good place to go out and start editing. No one source of information will be able to tell you everything about the art, craft, and job requirements of an editor, but, by now, you should have a solid handle on most of the basics. In this chapter we will augment our list of topics by addressing a hodgepodge of additional material, terms, concepts, and advice that will serve to flesh out your understanding even more. Learning from a book is an excellent way to start wrapping your brain around the editing process, but there is no replacement for on-the-job training. Finish this last chapter and start putting your knowledge into practice. The fun and satisfaction is to be found in the editing process itself, so get ready to go to work.

Additional Editing Terms

Parallel Editing

Used primarily in fictional narrative filmmaking, **parallel editing** (also known as **cross cutting**) calls for a special construction where two plot lines of the story's action are inter-cut with one another. In other words, a portion of one plot line is shown, then the sequence shifts over to showing the other plot line, which, in the film world, is supposed to be happening simultaneously. This technique proves especially effective during an action sequence — a race against time usually. Often, the pace of the piece gets more "frantic" as the two story lines unfold and get closer to the goal of the drama or suspense. This can be achieved by making the subsequent shots in the sequence of a shorter and shorter duration. The frenetic energy of the cuts carries over to the audience member who is feeling the urgency of this pacing and the race against time.

Montage

The term **montage** has several meanings when used in relation to motion picture editing. For the French, the word simply describes the act of assembling the film, which is the job of the editor. For many involved in Soviet silent cinema of the 1920s, it emerged as the Montage Theory of editing, which is a belief that two unrelated images can be edited together to generate a new thought, idea, or emotion in the mind of the viewer. An example presented earlier in this book tells of a young couple announcing their wedding engagement in shot A, which is then followed by an image of a prisoner with a ball-and-chain around his ankle in shot B. A viewer might get the idea that the filmmakers are equating marriage with a prison term.

The more widely applied meaning of montage today involves a series of quick cuts, usually accompanied by music, that show a condensed version of action over time. In a teen comedy it could be a series of shots showing the friends getting ready for the prom; in an action movie it could be a series of shots showing the elite fighting team going through tough training; in a romance it could be a series of shots showing a young couple going out on dates falling more and more in love with one another. A montage in this sense serves a useful purpose by condensing plot points that might otherwise unfold across a day, several weeks, or even years, into a shorter, more manageable duration.

Multi-camera Editing

Most fictional narrative filmmaking is accomplished with just one camera. The shots described earlier in this book are arranged, lit, and blocked for the one camera used to record those actions. There is a practice, however, where multiple cameras are used on set to shoot different angles of the same action getting two differing shots of coverage while the actors perform the action one time on one take. This method of using multiple cameras is very popular with recording studio-bound situation comedies for television, soap operas, reality programming, live theatre, and musical performances.

The beauty of multi-camera editing is that all of your source footage matches (usually according to matching **timecode**), and a cut at any point will have a corresponding continuous frame to cut to from another camera angle. Most professional digital non-linear editing software have a built-in process for matching up all of your camera source footage. As a result, you have the option of cutting to any camera angle at any point in time, much like a television studio director in the control room has the option of doing switching from camera A to camera C to camera B, and so on. Because the audio was also recorded as one, unbroken track during the performance, all of the camera images should match up perfectly while playing over the one source of audio.

Additional Editing Terms

Sync Sound and Counting Time

The term **sync** (short for synchronicity) has been used in filmmaking for a very long time. It usually refers to the synchronicity between the picture track of the film and the sound track(s). If there is a mismatch in the sync, then the words are not heard at the same time as the actor's mouth moves to say those words. Achieving and maintaining sync is a very important aspect of editing film and video.

As you know, emulsion film motion pictures are shot with a camera that only captures the pictures on a strip of light-sensitive flexible plastic. The audio is recorded by a separate device (formerly reel-to-reel ¼ magnetic tape, but now chiefly on digital recorders). These separate elements of picture and sound are then captured onto the computer and "married" together or "synched up" for the editing process. That is why we use the slate clapsticks to mark the "sync" point for the film image and the audio recording. Video cameras are capable of recording both picture and sound tracks to the one tape at the same time. These elements then come off the tape into your editing computer system already in sync, but it is still your responsibility to keep them in sync while you edit.

Without getting too technical, matching frame rates are required for the syncing of emulsion film and its recorded audio (24 frames per second or 24 fps). The same holds true for video (PAL = 25 fps and NTSC ≈ 30 fps). The next unifying factor is time. Film strips use frames and perforations to keep track of time but videotape, having no perforations, uses a special track on the tape that counts time according to hours, minutes, seconds, and frames (often appearing as 01:00:00:00). So for PAL projects on your editing software, you would be able to watch 25 separate frames in one second and for NTSC projects you would be able to see 30, but they go by your eye so quickly in one second that you really do not get to distinguish one from another.

Timecode is the counting scheme, or the clock, that most video editing software uses to keep time for frame rate playback and for keeping sync. The picture information and the audio information (when they come from the same tape source) will have the same matching timecode frame for frame. As an example, this is also how you know when you have completed your thirty-second commercial advertisement video (the timecode for your sequence may read, 00:00:30:00 if you started at the zero mark).

Making Your Way into the World of Editing

Tools vs. Skills

Film editing has been around for over one hundred years and video tape editing for about forty. Computer-aided or digital non-linear editing is the new kid on the block having its origins around 1990. The one thing all of these techniques/tools have in common is that they are means of assembling a story of some kind to be shown to an audience. The editors, over the years, have been the skilled craftspeople, technicians, and storytellers. The tools they have used have simply been a means to an end.

Today, in the computer age, the tools are different, but the skills of the person using them remain the same, or at least they should. Many people get lost in the nuances of the latest editing software and they separate the importance of their storytelling abilities from their knowledge of the computer's functionality. Or worse, they get so caught up in learning the latest bell or whistle in a specific editing application that they forget their primary goal as a storyteller. No one should confuse button-clicking abilities with solid editing skills.

There is a wide variety of computer-aided video editing software applications available on the market today. Several are of professional grade quality and are used by high-end, post-production facilities, television networks, movie studios, and the like. Many are geared for more in-home use and have fewer capabilities. Knowing how to use several of these applications will benefit the fledgling editor. Knowing one is a great start, but knowing more about using several from the high end is going to expand your job prospects considerably. The important thing to remember is that no matter what tool you end up using to perform the actual edit, you are the creative force behind the story forged.

Digital Workflow

The power, flexibility, and relative convenience that computer-aided digital non-linear editing has brought to the world of visual media creation are undeniable. It is not all fun and games, however. There is a responsibility, often placed upon the editor's shoulders, to be organized and knowledgeable about file types, media assets, and interoperability of various software applications. This creation, storage, and sharing of video and audio materials is generally referred to as **workflow**. It is increasingly rare for post-production workflows to incorporate **analog** source materials (like physical strips of motion picture film prints or analog video tape). Most independent software users and post-production facilities are now deep into the digital workflow, where all video and audio elements needed for a story are created, stored, used, and authored as digital files.

Not every version of digital video editing software uses the same types of files and not everyone encodes, stores, or accesses these files in the same way. A modern editor, in addition to being a great storyteller, must also be knowledgeable about these file types, feel comfortable with general computer operations, and understand media drives and folder hierarchies.

The user assigned details can also make a huge difference in how smooth the work-flow becomes. Naming conventions differ from place to place, but logic dictates that developing a sensible and concise method for naming projects, bins, sequences, clips, folders, graphics, source tapes, etc., is essential. With clarity in your names and organization to your raw, digital materials, you are already well on your way to a more comfortable digital workflow for the life of your editing project.

Digital Workflow

The Role of an Assistant Editor

Like many trades, guilds, and artisans over the centuries, knowledge is passed down from the more experienced editor to the apprentice or assistant editor. One day the assistant knows enough and has proven herself skilled enough to branch out on her own and become a full-blown editor in her own right. Many who start out in the field of video editing get their first job as an assistant editor and work their way up from there.

Responsibilities for assistants can vary widely depending on the type of show produced, the size of the budget, the type of post facility, and so forth. Generally speaking the assistant is assigned to an editor or an edit suite (the physical room where the editing takes place). They may be responsible for acquiring the raw master tapes of footage, setting up a project in the editing software, capturing the picture and sound files onto the computer and media drives, organizing the bin or folder structure within the project, and helping the editor output any final versions of the edited program for approval copies or eventual mastering of the completed product.

There are numerous nitty-gritty details that go along with any editing facility such as standardized naming conventions, particular media formats or media drive allocations, and so forth. The assistant editor works with others behind the scenes, as well as in front, to keep the post-production workflow smooth and easy for the editor so that he or she can perform the edit as free from stress or worry as possible thereby focusing on the storytelling aspect of the job and less on the organization and technical elements. Exposure to both sides of the editing process is a great training ground for the assistant, and he or she will be in good position to transition into the editor's chair when the time comes.

In Conclusion

No matter what computer software you end up using to perform your digital video edit, remember that you are the editor and the software is just the tool that helps you execute your decisions. As an editor you are, usually, the last creative person to touch the visual and auditory components of a project (musical scoring and audio track mixing come after picture lock) and as such, you have an incredible opportunity to help form or re-form the story told. Whatever you end up cutting, you should strive to combine your picture and sound elements in the best way possible. The shot choices you select, the rhythm and pacing of the individual edits, and the transition choices you make should all serve the story well and keep the viewing audience engaged, informed, and entertained. In the end, the grammar of the edit is the underlying language used to sew it all together.

End of Chapter Seven Review

1. Parallel editing cuts two, simultaneous story plot lines together so that concurrent action can be seen by the viewer at one time during the program. Usually done for action sequences.

2. Montage editing calls for a series of quick cuts, or a series of shots that condense actions across time into a short sequence usually accompanied by appropriate music.

3. Multi-camera editing allows you to edit footage of the same event captured by several cameras all at the same time. Useful for sports events, rock concerts, soap operas, and staged situation comedy television programs.

4. Timecode from original tape sources allows you to maintain sync between your picture and sound tracks within your edited sequence.

5. Do not let the complexity of video editing software move you away from your solid skills and good decision-making abilities as an editor.

6. Become familiar and comfortable with the workflow involved around managing digital media assets and the creation of computer-based video edits.

7. An assistant editor performs a variety of important and necessary tasks that help make the entire post-production process possible for the editor. Assisting an established editor is a great way to learn while you work and to become recommended when a new job comes along for you.

Glossary

30 degree rule—A cousin to the 180 degree rule, this rule decries that when recording coverage for a scene from differing camera angles within the film set, the camera should be moved around the 180 degree arc at least 30 degrees from one shot to the next to create enough variation on the angle-on-action so that the two different shots will edit together and appear different enough in their framing.

4:3—The aspect ratio for standard definition television. Four units wide by three units tall — more square in its visual presentation than the more modern high definition 16:9 video display.

180 degree line—The imaginary line established by the sight lines of talent within a shot that determines where the 180 degree arc of safe shooting is set up for the camera coverage of that scene. The camera should not be moved to the opposite side of this action line because it will cause a reversal in the established screen direction. See also 180 Degree Rule, Axis of Action, and Sight Line.

180 degree rule—In filmmaking, an imaginary 180 degree arc, or half circle, is established on one side of the shooting set once the camera first records an angle on the action in that space. All subsequent shots must be made from within that same semi-circle. Since screen direction, left and right, for the entire scene is established, the camera may not photograph the subject from the other side of the circle without causing a reversal in the screen direction.

16:9—The aspect ratio for high definition video. Sixteen units wide by nine units tall — a widescreen display is generated.

Act (noun)—In long form programming (feature films, episodic television, etc.) the "story" is broken down into several major sections known as acts. In fictional narrative filmmaking, a story will traditionally have three acts loosely termed the set-up, the confrontation, and the resolution.

Action—What the director calls out to signify that the acting for the shot being recorded should begin.

Action line—The imaginary line established by talent's sight line used to dictate from where on the film set the camera may be placed for coverage shooting.

ADR (automatic dialogue replacement)—A process where actors record lines of dialogue in a recording studio. Used to replace poor quality or all together missing production audio. An editor may then use these clean recordings for the actual edit.

Ambience (sound)—The general background sounds of any location where a scene for a film is shot. Examples: school cafeteria, football game arena, subway car.

Analog—Not digital in nature. Composed of or designed with a more free-form variant not specifically limited to a single, quantifiable range.

Angle on action—The angle from which a camera views the action on the film set.

Angle of incidence—The angle from which incident light falls upon a film set. A single lighting fixture directly overhead will have a 90 degree (from horizon) angle of incidence.

Angle of view—The field of view encompassed by the light gathering power of a film lens. A wide angle lens has a wide angle of view. A telephoto lens has a narrower angle of view on the world.

Aperture—In motion picture equipment terms, the aperture refers to the iris or flexible opening of the camera lens that controls how much or how little light is used to expose the image inside the camera. A wide aperture or iris setting lets in a larger amount of light. A smaller aperture lets in less light. On many camera lenses, the aperture can also be fully "stopped down" or closed all the way for total darkness on the image.

Artificial light—Any light generated by a man-made device such as a film light, a desk lamp, or a neon sign.

Aspect ratio—The numerical relationship between the dimensions of width and height for any given visual recording medium. In the example 16:9, the first number, 16, represents the units of measure across the width of a high-definition video frame. The second number, 9, represents the same units of measure for the height of the same frame.

Assemble edit—The phase during the post-production process where an editor first assembles the raw footage into a basic story structure.

Assistant editor—A support position within a post-production environment. The duties and responsibilities of an AE change with the complexity of the program edited, the budget, and the facility in which the edit is completed. General tasks include capturing and organizing footage within an editing project, attending to the chief editor's needs, authoring proof copies for review and approval, etc.

Atmosphere (sound)—The general background sounds of any location where a scene for a film is shot. Examples: school cafeteria, football game arena, subway car.

Atmospherics—Any particulates suspended in the air around a film set or location, such as fog or mist or dust, which will cumulatively obscure the distant background.

Attention—The direction in which a character faces within the film space. The attention of a character may be drawn by another character, an inanimate object, or anything that draws his or her attention. An imaginary line connects the eyes of the character and the object of their attention and, most often, the audience will trace this line to also see what the character sees. See also Sight Lines.

Audio mix—The process of blending together the many different audio tracks used in an edited program such that their levels (volumes) work appropriately together. Spoken dialogue, voice-over narration, music, sound effects, etc., are all blended so they sound good with one another under the picture track.

Axial edit—Cutting two shots together that view the subject from the exact same angle on action but only change the magnification of the subject. See also Cut-In and Punching-In.

Axis of action—The invisible line established by talent sight lines that helps establish what side of the action the camera can record coverage for that scene. The camera should not be moved to the opposite side of this action line because it will cause a reversal in the established screen direction. See 180 Degree Rule, Sight Line, and Imaginary Line.

Background—The zone within a filmed frame that shows the deep space farther away from camera. Most often the background is out of focus, but serves to generate the ambience of the location.

Back light—A light used on a film set placed behind the talent but pointed at their backside. It generally serves to help separate the body from the background by providing a rim or halo of light around the edges of the body, head, and hair.

Back timing—Laying in audio from a known and desired end point with an uncertain start point in your program.

Beat—A moment in time. A pause of no precise timing but appropriate for the needs of the edited piece. When strung together, several beats can account for the editor's gut instinct in proper timing of shots, titles, transition effects, and so on.

Binocular vision (human visual system)—Having two eyes located at the front of the head. The slight distance between the two eyes causes the human to see nearby objects from two distinct vantage points. The brain then combines the two distinct images into one picture where the overlapping elements take on a three-dimensional aspect.

Blocking—The movement of talent within the film space and the corresponding movement, if any, of the camera to follow the actions of the moving talent.

Boom arm—Deriving its name from the armature on a sailing ship's mast, a boom arm is used to swivel and extend the camera's placement to get sweeping shots or keep the camera buoyant without a tripod directly beneath it.

Boom operator (audio recording)—The crew member whose job it is to hold and manipulate the audio recording microphone suspended from a long, telescoping pole usually over the heads of the acting talent.

Break frame—When a recorded object accidentally moves to the edge of the frame and falls outside the visible area of the image.

B-roll—Any footage captured at a location that shows the environment and other details or non-specific visual aspects of an area or process that does not involve the principle subject of focus or main talent. Often used with news reporting while a reporter speaks over the imagery.

Business—Any busy work performed by an actor with their hands while acting in a scene.

Butt-cut—A straight edit between two picture frames in film or video with no transition effect such as a dissolve, wipe, or fade.

Camera angle—The angle at which a camera views a particular scene. Camera angles can be based on horizontal camera positioning around the subject or vertical camera positioning below or above the subject.

Camera person/camera operator—The person, man or woman, who physically handles the camera during the shooting. The main responsibility is to maintain proper framing and composition and to verify good focus.

Camera set-up—A place on the film set where a camera is positioned to record a shot. Each time the camera is physically moved to a new position it is considered a new camera set-up.

Camera support (tripods, etc.)—Any device or piece of film equipment that is used to support the motion picture camera. Tripods, dollies, car mounts, etc., are all examples of various kinds of camera support.

Canted angle—See also Dutch Angle.

Charge-coupled device (CCD)—The electronic light sensor built into most video cameras that turns light wave energy into electronic voltages. These voltages get recorded as brightness and color values on a tape or hard drive in the camera.

Chiaroscuro—Italian for light/dark. The term is used in the visual arts to talk about the high contrast ratio between light areas of a frame and dark areas. Filmmakers, as well as painters, use this technique to show or hide certain visual elements within their frames.

Clapper board—This is the visual record of the shot which is to be filmed. On the clapper board is marked the scene and the take number, together with other information about the shooting. The sound of the board "clapped" together is the point at which sound and vision are synchronized together during post-production. If a board is clapped it indicates that sound and vision are being recorded. If the board is held open it indicates that vision only is being recorded. If the board is shown upside down it shows that it was recorded at the end of the shot and is called an "end board." An end board can be also either clapped or mute. See also Slate.

Clean single—A medium shot to a close-up that contains body parts of only one person even though other characters may be part of the recorded scene.

Clip—Any piece of film or segment of digital video media file that will be used in an edited sequence.

Close-up shot—Any detail shot where the object of interest takes up the majority of the frame. Details will be magnified. When photographing a human being, the bottom of frame will just graze the top part of their shoulders and the top edge of frame may just cut off the top part of their head or hair.

Color bars—In video, these are the thick, colored vertical lines that are recorded first on a tape. They are used to calibrate or "line up" the editing machines, so that each time a picture is copied the color is the same. The colors are, from the left of the screen, white, yellow, cyan, green, magenta, red, blue, and black.

Color temperature—Often referenced on the degrees Kelvin scale, color temperature is a measurement of a light's perceived color when compared to the color of a "perfect black body" exposed to increasing levels of heat. The color temperature for film lighting is generally accepted as around 3200 degrees Kelvin. Sunlight is generally accepted as around 5600 degrees Kelvin. The lower numbers appear warm orange/amber when compared to "white" and the higher numbers appear cool blue.

Complex shot—Any shot that involves talent movement and movement of the camera (pan or tilt).

Composition—In motion picture terms, the artful design employed to place objects of importance within and around the recorded frame.

Continuity—In motion picture production terms: (1) Having actors repeat the same script lines in the same way while performing similar physical actions across multiple takes, (2) making sure that screen direction is followed from one camera set-up to the next, and (3) in post-production, the matching of physical action across a cut point between two shots of coverage for a scene.

Contrast—The range of dark and light tonalities within a film frame.

Contrast ratio—The level of delineation between strong areas of dark and strong areas of light within a film frame as represented in a ratio of two numbers — Key + Fill:Fill.

Coverage—Shooting the same action from multiple angles with different framing at each camera set-up; for example, a dialogue scene between two people may require a wide, establishing shot of the room, a tighter two-shot of both players, clean singles of each actor, reciprocal over-the-shoulder shots favoring each actor, cut-aways of hands moving, the clock on the wall, etc.

Crab—When a dolly moves the camera sideways or parallel to the movement/action recorded. The camera lens is actually perpendicular to the subjects most often.

Crane—Much like the large, heavy machinery used in construction, a crane on a film set may raise and move camera or have large lighting units mounted to it from high above the set.

Critical focus—As with the human eye, there can be only one plane or physical slice of reality that is in sharpest focus for the motion picture camera. The plane of critical focus is this slice of space in front of the lens that will show any object within that plane to be in true focus; for example, when recording a person's face in a medium close-up their eyes should be in sharpest focus. When the eyes are in sharpest focus then the plane of critical focus has been placed at the same distance away from the lens as the actor's eyes.

Cross cutting—The process of film construction where one plot line of action is inter-cut with another, potentially related plot line such that the audience is given an alternating taste of each one through a single scene. See also Parallel Editing.

Cross fade—An audio treatment applied to audio edits where the end of one piece of audio is faded down under the rising audio level of the next piece of sound.

Cross the line—Based on the concept inherent to the action line or 180 degree rule, this expression refers to accidentally moving the camera across the line and recording coverage for a scene that will not match established screen direction when edited together. See also Jump the Line.

Cut—An edit point (noun). To edit a motion picture (verb).

Cut away (verb)—Editing out of one shot to another shot that is different in subject matter from the previous one, e.g., "cut away from the postman coming through the gate to the dog inside the house, waiting."

Cut-away (noun)—Any shot recorded that allows a break from the main action within a scene. The editor will place a cut-away into an edited scene of shots when a visual break is necessary or when two other shots from the primary coverage will not edit together smoothly.

Cut-in—A tighter shot taken either with a long focal length lens or a closer camera position but along the same lens axis as the original wider shot. See also Axial Edit or Punching-In

Daylight balance—Film and video cameras may be biased toward seeing the color temperature of daylight as "white" light. When they are set this way, they have a daylight balance.

Degrees Kelvin—The scale used to indicate a light source's color temperature, ranging roughly from 1000 to 20,000. Red/orange/amber colored light falls from 1000 to 4000 and bluish light falls from 4500 on up to 20,000.

Depth—The distance from camera receding into the background of the set or location. The illusion of three-dimensional deep space on the two-dimensional film plane.

Depth of field (DOF)—In filmmaking terms, the depth of field refers to a zone, some distance from the camera lens, where any object will appear to be in acceptable focus to the viewing audience. The depth of field lives around the plane of critical focus, it appears one-third in front of and two-thirds behind the point of critical focus instead of centered equally. Any object outside the depth of field will appear blurry to the viewer. The depth of field may be altered or controlled by changing the camera to the subject distance or by adding light to or subtracting light from the subject.

Developing shot—Any shot that incorporates elaborate talent movement — a zoom, a pan or tilt, and a camera dolly.

Diegetic—Generated by something within the film world, usually associated with sound elements in a fictional motion picture; for example, a song playing on a juke box in a diner.

Director of photography (DP, DOP)—The person on the film's crew who is responsible for the overall look of a motion picture project's recorded image. He or she helps in planning the angles, composition, and movement of the camera as well as design details like color palettes, textures, and lighting schemes.

Dirty single—A medium shot to a close-up that contains the main person of interest for the shot that also contains some visible segment of another character who is also part of the same scene. The clean single is made "dirty" by having this sliver of another's body part in the frame.

Dissolve—A treatment applied to the visual track of a program at an edit point. While the end of the outgoing shot disappears from the screen, the incoming shot is simultaneously resolving onto the screen.

Dolly—Traditionally, any wheeled device used to move a motion picture camera around a film set either while recording or in between takes. A dolly may be three or four wheeled, ride on the floor or roll (with special wheels) along straight or curved tracks, or have a telescoping or booming arm that lifts and lowers camera.

Domestic cut-off—The outer ten percent of transmitted picture information that is cut off at the outside edges of a cathode ray tube (CRT) television set and not viewable by the in-home audience. This phenomenon should be taken into account when composing a shot for a project that will be broadcast on television.

Dutch angle/Dutch tilt—In filmmaker terms, any shot where the camera is canted or not level with the actual horizon line. The Dutch angle is often used to represent a view of objects or actions that are not quite right, underhanded, diabolical, or disquieting. All horizontal lines within the frame go slightly askew diagonally and as a result any true vertical lines will tip in the same direction.

Edit—The actual cut point between two different shots (noun). To assemble a motion picture from disparate visual and auditory elements (verb).

End frame—Any time the camera has been moving to follow action, the camera should come to a stop before the recorded action ceases. This clean, static frame will be used by the editor to cut away from the moving shot to any other shot that would come next. Moving frames cut to static frames is a very jarring visual cut and this static end frame helps prevent this mistake.

Establishing shot—Traditionally the first shot of a new scene in a motion picture. It is a wide shot that reveals the location where the immediately following action will take place. One may quickly learn place, rough time of day, rough time of year, weather conditions, historical era, etc., by seeing this shot.

Exposure—In motion picture camera terms, it is the light needed to create an image on the recording medium (either emulsion film or a video light sensor). If you do not have enough light you will under expose your image and it will appear too dark. If you have too much light you will overexpose your image and it will appear too bright.

Exterior—In film terms, any shot that has to take place outside.

Eye light—A light source placed somewhere in front of talent that reflects off the moist and curved surface of the eye. Sometimes called the "life light," this eye twinkle brings out the sparkle in the eye and often informs an audience that the character is alive and vibrant. Absence of the eye light can mean that a character is no longer living or is hiding something, etc.

Eye-line—The imaginary line that traces across the screen from a talent's eyes to some object of interest. See also Sight Line.

Eye-line match—When shooting clean single coverage for a two-person dialogue scene, the eyes of the two characters should be looking off frame in the direction of where the other character's head or face would be. Even though both actors may not be sitting next to one another as they were in the wider two-shot, the eye-line of each "looking" at the other must match from shot to shot so there is consistency in the edited scene.

Eye trace—The places on a screen that attract the interest of a viewer's eyes. As the motion picture plays on the screen the audience will move their focus around the composition to find new pieces of information.

Fade—A treatment of an edit point where the screen transitions from a solid color to a full visible image or from a fully visible image into a frame of solid color.

Fade-in (fade up)—Transitioning from a solid black opaque screen to a fully visible image.

Fade-out (fade down)—Transitioning from a fully visible image to a solid black opaque screen.

Fill light—A light of lesser intensity than the key light. It is used to help control contrast on a set but most often on a person's face. It is "filling" in the shadows caused by the dominant key light.

Film gauge—In the world of emulsion film motion pictures, the physical width of the plastic film strip is measured in millimeters (i.e., 16mm, 35mm). This measurement of film width is also referred to as the film's gauge.

Film space—The world within the film, both currently presented on screen and "known" to exist within the film's reality.

Fine cut—A later stage in the editing process where the edited program is very near completion. Any further changes will be minor.

Fisheye lens—A camera lens whose front optical element is so convex (or bulbous like the eye of a fish) that it can gather light rays from a very wide span. The resulting image formed while using such a lens often shows a distortion in the exaggerated expansion of physical space, object sizes, and perspective.

Flashback—A device in film construction that jumps the narrative from the present time of the story to an earlier time. Usually used to explain how the current circumstances came about.

Flash pan—A very quick pan action that blurs the image across the film or video frame. Often used in pairs as a way to transition out of one shot and into the next.

Focal length—The angle of view that a particular lens can record. It is a number, traditionally measured in millimeters (mm), that represents a camera lens' ability to gather and focus light. A lower focal length number (i.e., 10mm) indicates a wide angle of view. A higher focal length number (i.e., 200mm) indicates a more narrow field of view where objects further from the camera appear to be magnified.

Focus—The state where objects viewed by the camera appear to be sharply edged, well-defined, and show clear detail. Anything out of focus is said to be blurry.

Foley—A sound recording practice where "artists" make noises in a studio while they watch the edited motion picture. The sounds they record will replace or augment the sound effects of the film like footsteps, leather creaks, door knob jiggles, and so on.

Following focus—If a subject moves closer to or further away from the camera but stays within the film frame, often the camera assistant or camera operator must manually control the focus of the recording lens to keep the moving subject in clear, crisp focus. If the subject at the plane of critical focus moves away from that plane and outside the corresponding depth of field, they will get blurry unless the camera assistant follows focus.

Footage—The raw visual material with which the editor works. It is a general name given to the recorded images on the film or video tape that were created during production.

Foreground—The zone within a filmed frame that starts near the camera's lens but ends before it reaches a more distant zone where the main action may be occurring. Any object that exists in the foreground of the recorded frame will obscure everything in the more distant zones out to the infinity point.

Foreshortening—In the visual arts, it is a way that three-dimensional objects are represented on the two-dimensional plane. When pictured from a certain view or perspective, the object may appear compressed and/or distorted from its actual shape.

Fourth wall—In fictional narrative filmmaking, this term means the place from where the camera objectively observes the action on the film set. Since it is possible for the camera to record only three of the four walls within a film set, the fourth wall is the space on set where the camera lives and it is from that privileged place where it observes the action.

Frame—The entire rectangular area of the recorded image with zones of top, bottom, left, right, and center.

Front lighting—Any lighting scheme where lights come from above and almost directly behind the camera recording the scene. Talent, when facing toward the camera, will have an overall even lighting that often causes a flatness to their features.

Geared head—A professional piece of camera support used on dollies, cranes, and tripods that has two spinning geared wheels that allow for very fluid vertical and horizontal movements of the camera. The camera operator must manually crank each gear wheel to maintain the appropriate framing.

Gel—Heat-resistant sheet of flexible plastic film that contains a uniform color. Used to add a "wash" of color on a film set: For example, if the feeling of sunset is required for a shot, an orange/yellow gel can be placed between the lights and the set to give the impression of a warmer sunset color.

Golden hour—The moments just after direct sunset but before the ambient light in the sky fades to nighttime darkness. Filmmakers often appreciate the visual quality the soft top light of dusk creates on exterior scenes. Sometimes called the magic hour.

Grip—A film crew member whose job it is to move, place, and tweak any of the various pieces of film equipment used for support of camera, lighting units, or devices used to block light, among other duties. A special dolly grip may be used to rig the dolly tracks and push or pull the dolly/camera during the recording of a shot.

Handheld—Operating the motion picture camera while it is supported in the hands or propped upon the shoulder of the camera operator. The human body acts as the key support device for the camera and is responsible for all movement achieved by the camera during the recording process.

Hard light—A quality of light defined by the presence of strong, parallel rays emitted by the light source. Well-defined, dark shadows are created by hard light.

Head—The common film term for the beginning of a shot, especially during the post-production editing process.

Head room—The free space at the top of the recorded frame above the head of the talent. Any object may have head room. Too much head room will waste valuable space in the frame and not enough may cause your subject to appear cut off or truncated.

High angle shot—Any shot where the camera records the action from a vertical position higher than most objects being recorded; for example, the camera, looking out a third floor window of a house, records a car pulling into the driveway down below.

High definition (HD)—A reference to the increased image quality and wider frame size of the more recent digital video format. The increase in line resolution per frame (720 or 1080) increases the sharpness and color intensity of the playback image.

High-key lighting—A lighting style where there exists a low contrast ratio between the brightly lit areas and the dark areas of the frame. Overall, even lighting gives proper exposure to most of the set and characters within it. No real dark shadow regions and no real overly bright regions.

HMI—A film lighting fixture whose internal lamp burns in such a way it emits light that matches daylight/sunlight in color temperature (5500 – 6000 degrees Kelvin).

Hood mount—A device used to mount a tripod head and camera to the hood of a motor vehicle such that the occupants of the vehicle may be recorded while the vehicle is in motion. Often a large suction cup is employed to help secure the camera rig to the hood.

Horizon line—The distant line that cuts across a film frame horizontally. It is used to help establish the scope of the film space and helps define the top and bottom of the film world.

Imaginary line—The invisible line established by talent sight lines that helps establish what side of the action the camera can record coverage for that scene. The camera should not be moved to the opposite side of this action line because it will cause a reversal in the established screen direction. See also 180 Degree Rule, Sight Line, and Axis of Action.

Incoming picture—At a cut point, there is one shot ending and another beginning. The shot that is beginning after the cut point is the incoming picture.

Insert shot—Any shot inserted into a scene that is not part of the main coverage but relates to the story unfolding.

Interior—In film terms, any shot that has to take place inside.

Inter-titles—A title card or opaque graphic that appears on the screen to convey written information.

Iris—In motion picture equipment terms, the iris refers to the aperture of flexible opening of the camera lens that controls how much or how little light is used to expose the image inside the camera. Most modern video cameras use an electronic iris that has a thumb wheel that manually controls the setting for more or less light. Most high-end emulsion film and high definition lenses use an iris of sliding metal blades that overlap to make the aperture smaller or wider.

Jib arm—A piece of motion picture camera support equipment that allows the camera to move around a central fulcrum point, left/right/up/down/diagonal. It may be mounted onto tripod legs or on a dolly.

Jump cut—An anomaly of the edited film when two very similar shots of the same subject are cut together and played. A "jump" in space or time appears to occur that often interrupts the viewer's appreciation for the story.

Jump the line—Based on the concept inherent to the action line or 180 degree rule, this expression refers to accidentally moving the camera across the line and recording coverage for a scene that will not match established screen direction when edited together. See also Cross the Line.

Key light—The main light source around which the remaining lighting plan is built. Traditionally, on film sets, it is the brightest light that helps illuminate and expose the face of the main talent in the shot.

Kicker light—Any light that hits the talent from a three-quarter backside placement. It often rims just one side of the hair, shoulder, or jaw line.

L-cut—A cut point where the picture track and the sound track(s) are not joined exactly at the same frame. Picture track will last longer and play over the new incoming audio tracks, or a new picture track appears at the cut point and plays over the continuing audio from the outgoing shot. The clip segments around this edit will take on a horizontal "L" shape. See also Split Edit and Lapping.

Lapping (picture and sound)—The practice of editing where corresponding outgoing picture and sound tracks are not cut straight, but are staggered so one is longer and the other is shorter. The same treatment must therefore be given to the incoming picture and sound tracks. See Split Edit and L-Cut.

Legs—An alternate name for a camera tripod.

Lens axis—In motion picture camera terms, it is the central path cutting through the middle of the circular glass found in the camera's taking lens. Light traveling parallel to the lens axis is collected by the lens and brought into the camera exposing the recording medium. One can trace an imaginary straight line out of the camera's lens (like a laser pointer) and have it fall on the subject recorded. That subject is now placed along the axis of the lens.

Light meter—A device designed to read and measure the quantity of light falling on a scene or emitted from it. Often used to help set the level of exposure on the film set and, consequently, the setting on the camera's iris.

Line (line of action)—The imaginary line that connects a subject's gaze to the object of interest viewed by that subject; for example, a man, standing in the entry way of an apartment building, looks at the name plate on the door buzzer. The "line" would be traced from the man's eyes to the name plate on the wall. The next shot may be a big close-up of the name plate itself, giving the audience an answer to the question, "What is he looking at?"

Locked-off—The description of a shot where the tripod head pan and tilt controls are locked tight so there will be no movement of the camera. If it was necessary to make adjustments to the frame during shooting, the pan and tilt locks would be loosened slightly for smooth movement.

Log—Generally, all shots are written down while shooting. This list is called a shooting log. During the creation of an editing project, shots that are going to be used from original tape sources are also logged. After the entire sequence is completed, an edit decision list (an edit log) can also be created to keep track of the shots used and the timecodes associated with them.

Long shot—When photographing a standing human being, their entire body is visible within the frame and a good deal of the surrounding environment is also visible around them.

Look room/looking room/nose room—When photographing a person it is the space between their face and the farthest edge of the film frame. If a person is positioned frame left and is looking across empty space at frame right, then that empty space is considered the look room or nose room.

Looping (audio recording)—An audio post-production process where actors re-record better quality dialogue performance in a controlled studio. This new, clean audio track is then edited into the motion picture and appears in sync with the original picture.

Low angle shot—Any shot where the camera records the action from a vertical position lower than most objects recorded; for example, the camera, on a city sidewalk, points up to the tenth floor to record two men cleaning the windows.

Lower thirds—A title or graphic that appears as a superimposed visual element across the bottom lower third of the screen. Usually used to identify a person or place in a factual news piece or a documentary interview.

Low-key lighting—A lighting style where a large contrast ratio between the brightly lit areas and the dark areas of the frame exist; for example, film noir used low-key lighting to create deep, dark shadows and single source key lighting for exposure of principal subjects of importance.

Mastering—The process of creating the final version of an edited program that looks and sounds the best and will be used to create other versions for distribution.

Match dissolve—A dissolve between two shots whose visual elements are compositionally similar. Shape, color, mass, or brightness of the outgoing shot will dissolve into visually similar shape, color, mass, or brightness of the incoming shot.

Matching angles/shots (reciprocating imagery)—When shooting coverage for a scene, each camera set-up favoring each character being covered should be very similar if not identical. One should match the framing, camera height, focal length, lighting, and so forth. When edited together the "matching shots" will balance one another and keep the information presented about each character consistent.

Medium shot—When photographing a standing human being, the bottom of the frame will cut off the person around the waist.

Middle ground—The zone within a filmed frame where the majority of the important visual action will take place. Objects in the middle ground may be obscured by other objects in the foreground, but middle ground objects may then also obscure objects far away from camera in the background.

Monocular vision (camera lens)—A visual system in which only one lens takes in and records all data. The three-dimensional aspect of human binocular vision is not present in the monocular vision of the film or video camera.

Montage—A series of edits that show an event or events that happen over time but are condensed into a brief episode of screen time. It is usually edited to music.

MOS (minus optical stripe)—A term that describes a picture track that was recorded without any sound. This originated in the days of emulsion film.

Motivated light—Light, seen on a film set, that appears to be coming from some light source within the actual film world.

Natural light—Any light that is made by the sun or fire. Non-man-made sources.

Natural sound (nat sound)—Audio ambience or background sounds recorded on video tape at the time of the picture being recorded.

Natural wipe—Any large visual element that can move across and obscure the frame while recording a shot on a film set or location. This object naturally wipes the frame and blocks the view of the main subject or object of interest.

Negative space—An artistic concept wherein unoccupied or empty space within a composition or arrangement of objects also has mass, weight, and importance and is worth attention.

Neutral density filter—A device that reduces the amount of light entering a camera (density), but does not alter the color temperature of that light (neutral). It is either a glass filter that one can apply to the front of the camera lens or, with many video cameras, a setting within the camera's electronics that replicates the reduced light effect of neutral density filters.

Noddy—Any reaction shot used as a cut-away. Most often associated with news interviews and some documentary pieces, these shots of heads nodding are usually recorded after the main interview and are edited in to cover up audio edits.

Normal lens—A camera lens whose focal length closely replicates what the field of view and perspective might be on certain objects if these same objects were seen with human eyes.

Objective shooting—A style of camera operation where the talent never addresses the existence of the camera. The camera is a neutral observer not actively participating in the recorded event but simply acting as a viewer of the event for the benefit of the audience.

Outgoing picture—At a cut point, there is one shot ending and another beginning. The shot that is ending prior to the cut point is the outgoing picture.

Overexposed—A state of an image where the bright regions contain no discernable visual data but appear as glowing white zones. The overall tonality of this image may also be lacking in true "black" values so everything seems grey to white in luminance.

Overheads—Drawings or diagrams of the film set, as seen from above like a bird's-eye-view, that show the placement of camera, lighting equipment, talent, and any set furnishings, etc. These overheads will act as a map for each department to place the necessary equipment in those roughed-out regions of set.

Overlapping action—While shooting coverage for a particular scene, certain actions made by talent will have to be repeated from different camera angles and framings. When cutting the film together, the editor will benefit from having the talent making these repeated movements, or overlapping actions, in multiple shots so when the cut is made it can be made on the movement of the action from the two shots.

Over-the-shoulder (OTS) shot—A shot used in filmmaking where the back of a character's head and one of his shoulders occupy the left/bottom or right/bottom foreground and act as a "frame" for the full face of another character standing or seated in the middle ground opposite from the first character. This shot is often used when recording a dialogue scene between two people.

Overwrite—Mostly associated with video editing, an edit command that actually writes new frames of picture and sound over on top of, and replacing, existing video.

Pan—Short for panorama, the horizontal movement, from left to right or right to left, of the camera while it is recording action. If using a tripod for camera support, the pan is achieved by loosening the pan lock on the tripod head and using the pan handle to swivel the camera around the central pivot point of the tripod to follow the action or reveal the recorded environment.

Pan and scan—A process used in television broadcasting where an original wide-screen motion picture image is cropped down to fit into a 4:3 aspect ratio window (the screen size of SDTV) and slid or panned left and right to help maintain some degree of picture composition. If a widescreen image did not have the pan and scan treatment, it would have to have the letterbox treatment to show the entire widescreen aspect ratio inside the more-square 4:3 TV screen.

Pan handle—A tripod head with a horizontal pivot axis allows for the panning action of the camera either left or right. The pan handle is a stick or length of metal tubing that extends off the tripod head and allows the camera operator to control the rate of movement of the camera pan by physically pushing or pulling it around the central axis point of the tripod.

Parallel editing—The process of film construction where one plot line of action is inter-cut with another, potentially related plot line such that the audience is given an alternating taste of each one through a single scene. See also Cross Cutting.

Pedestal—A camera support device that has vertical boom and 360 degree free-wheel capabilities. Most often used on the floor of a television studio.

Picture lock—The phase of editing a motion picture where there will be no more additions to or subtractions from the picture track(s). From that point forward, the remaining audio construction and tweaking may take place.

Point-of-view—In filmmaking terms, any shot that takes on a subjective stance. The camera records exactly what one of the characters is seeing. The camera sits in place of the talent, and what it shows to the viewing audience is supposed to represent what the character is actually seeing.

Point source—A light source that is derived from a specific, localized instance of light generation/emission. A non-diffused light source.

Post-production—The phase of motion picture creation that traditionally happens after all of the live-action film or video is shot (production). Post-production can include picture and sound editing, title and graphics creation, motion effects rendering, color correction, musical scoring, mixing, etc.

Practical—A functional, on-set lighting fixture visible in the recorded shot's frame that may actually help illuminate the set for exposure: For example, a shot of a man sitting down at a desk at night. Upon the desk is a desk lamp whose light illuminates the face of the man.

Pre-production—The period of work on a motion picture project that occurs prior to the start of principal photography (production).

Glossary

Production—The period of work on a motion picture project that occurs while the scenes are recorded on film or video. This could be as short as a single day for a commercial or music video or last several months for a feature film.

Proscenium style—In theatre as well as motion pictures, a way to stage the action such that it is seen from only one direction. The audience, or in a film's case, the camera, views and records the action from only one angle.

Pulling focus—Camera lenses that have manual controls for the focus will allow a camera assistant or camera operator to move the plane of critical focus closer to the camera, therefore shifting what appears to be in sharp focus within the recorded frame. This is often done to shift focus from one farther object in the frame to one closer object within the frame.

Punching-in—See also Axial Edit and Cut-In.

Pushing focus—Camera lenses that have manual controls for the focus will allow a camera assistant or camera operator to move the plane of critical focus further away from the camera, therefore shifting what appears to be in sharp focus within the frame being recorded. This is often done to shift focus from a near object in the frame to one further away.

Rack focus—During the recording of a shot that has a shallow depth of field, the camera assistant or camera operator may need to shift focus from one subject in the frame to another. This shifting of planes of focus from one distance away from the camera to another is called racking focus.

Reaction shot—A shot in a scene that comes after some action or line of dialogue. The first shot is the catalyst for the reaction depicted in the second shot. It lets a viewer know how the other characters are reacting to the action, event, or dialogue just shown.

Reformat—Changing the shape, size, and sometimes frame-rate of a motion picture so that it will play on different sized screens or in different countries with alternate standards for motion picture display.

Reveal—Any time the filmmaker shows new, important, or startling visual information on the screen, either through camera movement, talent blocking, or edited shots in post-production. The reveal of information is the payoff after a suspenseful expectation has been established within the story.

Rim light—Any light source whose rays "rim" or "halo" the edges of a subject or an object on the film set, often set somewhere behind the subject.

Room tone—The sound of "silence" that is the underlying tone present in every room or environment where filming takes place. Most sound recordists will capture at least thirty seconds of room tone at every location where filming has occurred. Editors use this tone to fill in gaps of empty space on the audio tracks so it has a continuous level or tone throughout.

Rough cut—An initial stage of program editing that usually comes just after the assemble stage. The story is "roughed" out during this construction phase of the edit.

Rule of thirds—A common gauge of film frame composition where an imaginary grid of lines falls across the frame, both vertically and horizontally, at the mark of thirds. Placing objects along these lines or at the cross points of two of these lines is considered part of the tried and true composition of film images.

Running time—The actual time an entire edited program takes to play through from start to finish.

Safe action line—Related to the domestic cut-off phenomenon, the safe action line is found on many camera viewfinders and is used to keep the important action composed more toward the inner region of the frame. This prevents important action from being cut off.

Scene—A segment of a motion picture that takes place at one location. A scene may be comprised of many shots from different camera angles or just one shot from one camera set-up.

Screen direction—The direction in which a subject moves across or out of the frame; for example, a person standing at the center of frame suddenly walks out of frame left. The movement to the left is the established screen direction. When the next shot is cut together for the story, the same person must enter the frame from frame right, continuing their journey in the same screen direction — from the right to the left.

Sequence—A number of shots joined together that depict a particular action or event in a longer program. Sometimes likened to a scene, but a longer scene may have several key sequences play out inside of it.

Shooting ratio—The amount of material you shoot for a project compared to the amount of material that makes it into the final edit: For example, you shoot fourteen takes of one actor saying a line, but only use one of those takes in the final movie. You have a 14:1 shooting ratio for that one line of dialogue.

Shot—One action or event that is recorded by one camera at one time. A shot is the smallest building block used to edit a motion picture.

Shot list—A list of shots, usually prepared by the director during pre-production, that will act as a guide for what shots are required for best coverage of a scene in a motion picture project. It should show the shot type and may follow a number and letter naming scheme.

Shot-reverse-shot—A term applied to an editing style, where one shot of a particular type (medium close-up) is used on one character, then the same type of shot (medium close-up) is edited next to show the other character in the scene. You see the shot, reverse the camera, and see a matching shot of the other.

Side lighting—A method of applying light to a subject or film set where the lights come from the side, not above or below.

Sight line—The imaginary line that traces the direction in which a subject is looking on screen. Sometimes called a line of attention. Sight line also establishes the line of action and sets up the 180 degree arc for shooting coverage of a scene.

Silhouette—A special way of exposing a shot where the brighter background is correct in its exposure on film but the subject (in the middle ground or foreground) is underexposed and appears as a black shape with no detail but the edge shape.

Simple shot—Any shot that only contains minor talent movement but uses no zoom, no tilt/pan, no camera dolly, and no booming actions. Locked-off framing.

Slate (noun)—The clapboard used to identify the shot recorded. Often the name of the production, director, DP, the shooting scene, and the date are written on the slate. Using the clapboard sticks to make a "clapping" sound that will serve as a synchronization point of picture and sound tracks during the edit process (verb).

Slop edit—An assembly edit done very early on in the edit process where speed of creation overrides the precision of the actual cut points. The general structure of the story is hastily assembled.

Slow motion—Any treatment in film or video where the actual time of an event to occur is slowed down considerably so it lasts longer in screen time and more detail of the action can be analyzed.

Smash cut—An abrupt and often jarring transition between two contrasting actions that happen at different times or places.

Soft light—Any light that has diffused, non-parallel rays. Strong shadows are very rare if one uses soft light to illuminate talent.

Sound bridge—An audio treatment given to a cut point where either the sound of the outgoing shot continues underneath the new image of the incoming picture track or the new audio of the incoming shot begins to play before the picture of the outgoing shot leaves the screen.

Sound design—The process of building audio tracks that act to augment and enhance the physical actions seen on the screen and the sounds from the environments in which the story's action takes place. These sounds may be actual sounds or fabricated to generate a hyper-reality of the audio elements in a program.

Sound on tape (SOT)—Most often associated with the spoken word from news reporters or documentary interviewees. SOTs are the sound bites.

Sound recordist—The person on a film crew responsible for recording spoken dialogue, ambience, and room tone.

Splice—To cut two shots together (verb). Originated when actual film strips were taped or glued together to join them at an edit point. The actual cut point on a strip of film where two pieces are glued or taped together (noun).

Splicer—In film, the footage is physically cut with a small machine called a splicer and the pictures are "spliced" together with glue or special transparent tape.

Split edit—A cut point where the picture track and the sound track(s) are not joined exactly at the same frame. Picture track will last longer and play over the new incoming audio tracks, or a new picture track appears at the cut point and plays over the continuing audio from the outgoing shot. The clip segments around this edit will take on a horizontal "L" shape. See also L-Cut and Lapping.

Spot—Slang for a television commercial advertisement.

Spreader (tripod)—The three legs of a tripod are often attached to a rubber or metal device to keep the legs from splaying too far apart while the heavy camera sits atop the tripod head. This three-branched brace allows for greater stability, especially as the tripod legs are spread further and further apart to get the camera lower to the ground.

Staging—The placement of talent and objects within the film set.

Standard definition (SD)—A reference to the normal image quality and frame size of most televisions around the world during the twentieth century. Limitations in broadcast bandwidth, among other technological reasons, required a low resolution image of the 4:3 aspect ratio for television reception in the home.

Start frame—Any time the camera needs to move to follow action, the camera should begin recording, stay stationary for a few moments while the action begins, and then start to move to follow the action. The start frame is required by the editor of the film so the shot will have a static frame to start on at the beginning of the cut. Static frames cut to moving frames is a very jarring visual cut and this static start frame helps prevent this mistake.

Sticks—(1) An alternate name for a camera tripod and (2) the clapboard or slate used to mark the synchronicity point of picture and sound being recorded.

Storyboards—Drawings often done during pre-production of a motion picture that represent the best guess of what the ultimate framing and movement of camera shots will be when the film goes into production. The comic book like illustrations will act as a template for the creative team when principal photography begins.

Straight cut—An edit point where the picture track and sound track(s) are cut and joined at the same moment in time. See also Butt-Cut.

Subjective shooting—A style of camera operation where the talent addresses the camera straight into the lens (as in news broadcasting) or when the camera records exactly what a character is observing in a fictional narrative as with the point-of-view shot.

Suite—A small room in which editing machines are kept and used. The actual editing of the program will often occur in this private, dark, quiet room so the editor can stay focused on the footage and the sound elements without outside disturbances.

Superimposition—When an image of less than 100% opacity is placed on top of another image. This is like a dissolve that lasts for a longer time on screen.

Sync—Short for synchronicity. In film work, it refers to how the audio tracks play in corresponding time with the picture track. When you see the mouth move you hear the appropriate audio play at the exact same time.

Tail—The common film term for the end of a shot, especially during the post-production editing process.

Tail slate—Often used while recording documentary footage, a tail slate is the process of identifying the shot and "clapping" the slate after the action has been recorded but before the camera stops rolling.

Take—Each action, event, or dialogue delivery recorded in a shot may need to be repeated until its technical and creative aspects are done to the satisfaction of the filmmakers. Each time the camera rolls to record this repeated event is a "take." Takes are traditionally numbered starting at "one."

Taking lens—The active lens on a motion picture or video camera that is actually collecting, focusing, and controlling the light for the recording of the image. On certain models of emulsion film motion picture cameras there can be more than one lens mounted to the camera body. Most video cameras have but one lens and that would be the "taking" lens.

Talking head—Any medium close-up shot or closer that really just focuses on one person's head and shoulders. Usually associated with documentaries, news, and interview footage.

Three point lighting—A basic but widely used lighting method where you employ a key light for main exposure on one side of talent, a fill light to contrast control on the opposite side, and a back light for subject/background separation.

Tilt—The vertical movement, either down up or up down, of the camera while it is recording action. If using a tripod for camera support, the tilt is achieved by loosening the tilt lock on the tripod head and using the pan handle to swing the camera lens up or down to follow the vertical action or reveal the recorded environment.

Timecode—A counting scheme based on hours, minutes, seconds, and frames that is used to keep track of image and sound placement on video tapes and within computer-based digital video editing software.

Track in/out—Moving the camera into set or pulling camera out of set, usually atop a dolly on tracks. Also known as trucking in and trucking out.

Tracks/rail—Much like railroad tracks, these small-scale metal rails are used to smoothly roll a dolly across surfaces, either inside or outside, to get a moving shot.

Glossary

Tripod—A three-legged device, often with telescoping legs, used to support and steady the camera for motion picture shooting. The camera attaches to a device capable of vertical and horizontal axis movement called the tripod head, which sits atop the balancing legs.

Tripod head—The device, usually mounted on top of tripod legs, to which one attaches the camera. The head may have panning and tilting functionality.

Truck in/out—Moving the camera into set or pulling camera out of set, usually atop a dolly on tracks. Also known as tracking in and tracking out.

Tungsten balanced—Film and video cameras may be biased toward seeing the color temperature of tungsten lamps as "white" light. When they are set this way, they have a tungsten balance.

Two-shot—Any shot that contains the bodies (or body parts) of two people.

Underexposed—A state of an image where the dark regions contain no discernable visual data but appear as deep black zones. The overall tonality of this image may also be lacking in true "white" values so everything seems gray down to black in luminance.

Vanishing point—A long-established technique in the visual arts where opposing diagonal lines converge at the horizon line to indicate the inclusion of a great distance in the image's environment. It is an illusion used to help represent three-dimensional space on a two-dimensional surface.

Vari-focal lens—Another name for a "zoom" lens. A lens that has multiple elements that allow it to catch light from various focal lengths or angles of view on a scene.

Video format—Video tapes record electronic voltage fluctuations or digital bit data that represent picture and sound information. Video cameras are manufactured to record that data onto the tape in a particular way. The shape, amount of data, frame rate, color information, etc., that gets recorded is determined by the technologies inside the video camera. Examples include NTSC-525 line, PAL, HD-1080i, and HD-720p.

Visible spectrum—The zone in electro-magnetic energy waves that appears to our eyes and brains as colored light.

Voice-over narration—An edited program may require the voice of an unseen narrator who provides important information or commentary about the story that is unfolding. The voice is heard "over" the pictures and the Nats.

Voice slate—A practice used at the head of a shot after the camera is rolling and before the director calls "action." Often, a camera assistant will verbally speak the scene and take number to identify the audio data that may be recorded separately from the picture.

Whip pan—An extremely quick panning action that will cause severe motion blur on the recorded image. Often used to exit a scene and then quickly begin another at a different time or place.

Wipe—An editing transition where an incoming shot's image literally wipes the existing outgoing shot's image from the screen.

Workflow—A pre-planned organization of source material, edited assets, and completed programs. A charted distribution of post-production elements that should be known by all involved parties so that the job can work smoothly from start to finish.

Zoom lens—A camera lens whose multi-lens construction and telescoping barrel design allow it to gather light from a wide range or field of view and also from a very narrow (more magnified) field of view. The focal length of the lens is altered by changing the distances of the optical elements contained within the lens barrel itself. Most modern video cameras have built in optical zoom lenses that can be adjusted from wide to telephoto with the touch of a button.

Index